Essential Histories

The Mexican War
1846–1848

Essential Histories

The Mexican War
1846–1848

Douglas V. Meed

First published in Great Britain in 2002 by Osprey Publishing,
Elms Court, Chapel Way, Botley, Oxford OX2 9LP, UK
Email: info@ospreypublishing.com

ISBN 1 84176 472 8

Editor: Kate Targett
Design: Ken Vail Graphic Design, Cambridge, UK
Cartography by The Map Studio
Index by Alison Worthington
Picture research by Image Select International
Origination by Grasmere Digital Imaging, Leeds, UK
Printed and bound in China by L. Rex Printing Company Ltd.

02 03 04 05 06   10 9 8 7 6 5 4 3 2 1

For a complete list of titles available from Osprey Publishing
please contact:

Osprey Direct UK, PO Box 140,
Wellingborough, Northants, NN8 2FA, UK.
Email: info@ospreydirect.co.uk

Osprey Direct USA, c/o MBI Publishing,
PO Box 1, 729 Prospect Ave,
Osceola, WI 54020, USA.
Email: info@ospreydirectusa.com

www.ospreypublishing.com

Contents

Introduction

The war with Mexico was one of the most decisive conflicts in American history. For Mexico, the war was its greatest disaster. It was a bitter, hard-fought conflict that raged through the northern deserts of Mexico, the fever-ridden gulf cities, and the balmy haciendas of California, reaching its climax at the fabled Halls of Montezuma in Mexico City. Although the numbers of troops involved were not large by Napoleonic standards, the fighting was ferocious and deadly.

To Mexicans, the immediate cause of the war was the Texas problem. Texas had been a festering sore on the Mexican body politic for more than a decade. After Texas troops smashed the dictator Santa Anna's army at San Jacinto in March 1836, hoping to save his own life, Santa Anna granted independence to the rebellious province with the Treaty of Velasco. As a result, Texas maintained its status as an independent democratic republic for almost ten years. The Mexican government, however, repudiated Santa Anna's treaty and maintained that Texas continued to be a province of Mexico.

While campaigning for the American presidency in 1844, James K. Polk vowed to annex Texas and acquire California and all the lands in between, and the Mexican government feared a confrontation with their expansionist neighbor. When Polk was elected, in March 1845, and Texas was annexed in December of that year, Mexico threatened war.

It was not surprising then, that when Polk sent an emissary to Mexico City offering to

'Go west young men. Go west!' rang out the cry, as thousands began the trek toward the setting sun. They came by ship, by covered wagon, and some even crossed the continent on foot. When gold was discovered in California in 1848, the west was viewed as the new El Dorado. (The Church of Latter-day Saints Museum)

purchase that country's western lands, he was ignored. The American president was prepared to purchase Mexican territory, but he was also prepared, if necessary, to take it by force.

To add to the tension there was a dispute over the location of the southern boundary of Texas. The Texans claimed it was the Rio Grande River; the Mexicans said it was the Nueces River, in some places 140 miles further north.

In the spring of 1846, Polk sent troops to the area. An American army under General Zachary Taylor crossed the Nueces and headed south to the Rio Grande. At the same time a Mexican army crossed the Rio Grande and headed north to the Nueces. In late April the armies clashed in the first battle of the war.

An overconfident Mexican government declared war on the United States on 23 April 1846, believing that their experienced military forces could crush the impudent Americans and their minuscule regular army. This was to be a fatal mistake.

On 13 May 1846, the Congress of the United States declared war on Mexico after an address by President Polk in which he pronounced: 'American blood has been shed on American soil.' The war was greeted enthusiastically in the southern and western states but was bitterly opposed by many of the eastern and New England states, who believed the spoils of a gigantic land grab would result in an extension of slavery.

During the campaigns in northern Mexico, the American invaders fought pitched battles in fortified cities and mountain passes, bringing heavy casualties for both sides.

The western theater presented American troops with pitiless weather and semi-arid expanses of mountains and plains, where water was scant and raiding Indians plentiful. Trekking west was a logistical nightmare until the troops reached the fruitful land of California.

Colonel Alexander Doniphan with his Missouri Mounted Volunteers trekked south-west, captured Sante Fe, then drove

into Mexico, capturing Chihuahua City. Continuing deeper into enemy territory, he occupied Torreon before turning east to link up with Taylor's troops in Monterey.

Another expedition, led by Brigadier General Stephen Watts Kearny, conquered the northern territories of Mexico and then marched to the Pacific shores to help seize California. Meanwhile, American settlers in northern California were rising against the Mexican government and launched the Bear Flag Rebellion, aided by explorer John C. Fremont. After fighting several skirmishes,

Kearny's and Fremont's forces were combined with an American naval squadron to control all of California.

Often neglected in many accounts, the American Navy played a key part in the war. American flotillas dominated the Caribbean, the Gulf of Mexico, and the west coast of Mexico and California. The Navy performed yeoman duty in blockading ports, transporting troops, and providing naval gunfire in support of the army. The war, however, dragged on. General Winfield Scott proposed a seaborne invasion of Mexico that would drive inland to Mexico City, capture it and force a peace on a reluctant Mexican government.

The first American amphibious invasion force rowed ashore south of Vera Cruz in March 1847. Capturing the port after a massive bombardment by both land and sea, Scott moved inland. Fighting all the way, the Americans drove 200 miles over rugged

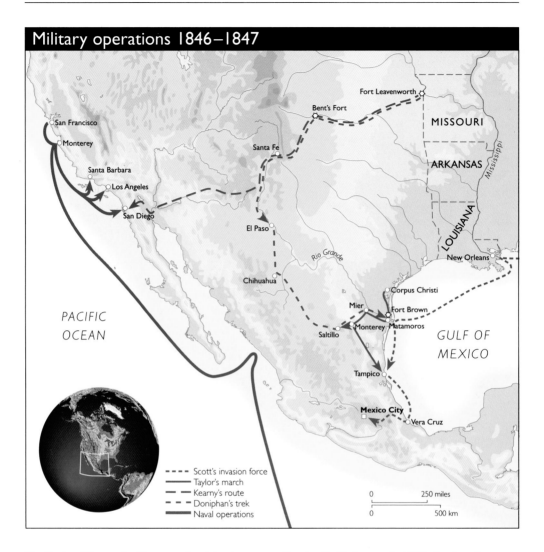

Military operations 1846–1847

Fort Leavenworth

Bent's Fort

MISSOURI

San Francisco

Monterey

Santa Fe

ARKANSAS

Santa Barbara

Los Angeles

San Diego

El Paso

LOUISIANA

New Orleans

Chihuahua

Rio Grande

Corpus Christi

Mier   Fort Brown

PACIFIC
OCEAN

Saltillo   Monterey Matamoros

GULF OF
MEXICO

Tampico

Mexico City

Vera Cruz

- - - - Scott's invasion force
——— Taylor's march
— — Kearny's route
- - - Doniphan's trek
——— Naval operations

0   250 miles

0   500 km

The Mexican War was fought on a continental scale. Kearny's march west from Ft. Leavenworth to San Diego stretched 2,000 miles. Colonel Doniphan's Missouri Volunteers headed west to Santa Fe, dipped south to El Paso del Norte, and on to Monterey and Matamoros. There they took a ship to New Orleans and then marched home to Missouri. In all, they covered 5,500 miles. From Fort Brown, Zachary Taylor's men penetrated 200 miles to Saltillo and 300 more to Tampico. Scott's troops sailed 550 miles, from the logistical center of the war effort in New Orleans to Matamoros. Reinforced there, Scott sailed another 500 miles, landing at Vera Cruz. Then he fought his way 250 miles south to Mexico City. To join the action, the United States Navy, based on the east coast, sailed down the South American coastline, rounded Cape Horn, and climbed another 7,500 miles to San Francisco.

terrain to Mexico City. To protect Scott's supply line, Texas Rangers fought a brutal war with Mexican guerrillas in which prisoners were few and atrocities many.

After winning battles before the Mexican capital at Contreras and Churubusco, Scott's army suffered heavy casualties at Molino del Rey before overcoming opposition. Then

Scott advanced on Mexico City. The climatic battle of the war was fought at Chapultepec Castle, where the Americans scaled the walls of the fortress and charged into Mexico City. With the occupation of their capital and their armies smashed, Mexican resistance was broken and Mexico was forced into a draconian peace in which they surrendered more than half their territory.

Much as the Spanish Civil War of 1936–39 was a prelude to the Second World War, the American war with Mexico became in many respects a precursor to the long and frightful American Civil War of 1861–65.

The victory over Mexico was clouded by the fact that the political and moral struggle between the American slave states and the industrializing North became greatly intensified. As abolitionists preached their doctrines to 'shake off the fetters of servitude,' Southern paranoia increased. Soon the Southern states would seek secession as their only alternative to domination by the North. In the words of Winston Churchill, the American Civil War was doomed to be ' the noblest and least avoidable of all the great mass conflicts.'

If, at the end of the war with Mexico, the Americans gained vast, near-empty territories, Mexicans were left with only a numbing grievance. 'Poor Mexico,' they complained, 'so far from God and so close to the United States.'

Chronology

1836 **21 April** A Texan army defeats Santa Anna at the battle of San Jacinto. Texas becomes an independent republic.

1845 **29 December** The United States annexes Texas. President Polk sends a negotiator to Mexico City in an effort to purchase Mexican western lands.

1846 **March** General Zachary Taylor and an American army land in Corpus Christi.
23 April Mexico declares war on the United States.
8–9 May General Taylor wins battles at Palo Alto and Resaca de la Palma.
13 May The United States declares war on Mexico.
12 June Great Britain and the United States reach a compromise on the boundaries of the Oregon Territory, thus averting a conflict.
14 June Bear Flag Rebellion. California declares independence from Mexico.
18 August General Stephen Kearny occupies Sante Fe.

20–24 September General Taylor wins battle of Monterey.

1847 **10 January** Commodore Stockton occupies Los Angeles.
22–23 February General Taylor wins the battle of Buena Vista.
1 March Doniphan occupies Chihuahua City.
29 March Vera Cruz surrenders to General Winfield Scott.
18 April General Scott wins battle of Cerro Gordo.
19–20 August General Scott wins battles at Contreras and Churubusco.
8 September General Scott wins battle of Molino del Rey.
13 September General Scott wins the climactic battle of the war at Chapultepec.
14 September General Scott enters Mexico City in triumph.

1848 **25 March** The Treaty of Guadalupe Hidalgo ends the war.

Different cultures collide

The struggle between the United States and Mexico exposed a massive economic, social, and political chasm between two diverse cultures separated by a common border.

The Americans, 20 million strong, were a hard-driving, egalitarian, vigorous people. They fervently believed the 'Manifest Destiny' of the United States was ordained by God to stretch from the Atlantic to the Pacific. Theirs was a society based on a democracy founded on British common law, the European Enlightenment, and a secular government.

Pitted against this dynamic force was an older, more traditional, aristocratic society of seven million Mexicans racked by endemic factionalism and revolt. Mexico had a received religion, structured castes and a monarchical-styled political system that was wont to pose as a democracy. It was a land divided by race, caste, and a massive economic gulf between rich landowners, with their palatial haciendas, and the mass of landless peasants. There was a burgeoning nationalism among the elite and a spirit of machismo resistance to invaders among many of the people, yet among the landless and the indigenous Indians, who had little stake in the country, there was apathy and indifference.

American relations with Spain were often less than cordial and Mexico's successful battle for independence had been welcomed by its neighbor to the north. After almost 300 years of putative rule, the Spanish frontier north of the Rio Grande was sparsely settled and economically unproductive. Catholic missions in Texas had been abandoned and the few scattered towns were inhabited by the Mestizos, the new blend of Spaniard and Indian who formed the largest race in Mexico. The curse of these Borderlands were the roaming bands of Apaches, Comanches, Kiowas, Kickapoos, and other predatory tribes, who swooped down on Mexican settlements

to loot and kill. A parsimonious Spanish government offered little help against these raiders, and the succeeding Mexican authorities offered even less.

In the twilight of their rule, the Spanish, viewing the wreckage of their northern frontier, where the raiding nomads had virtually depopulated Mexican settlements as far south as Chihuahua City, had what they believed to be a brilliant idea. They believed the voracious, land-hungry Americans might be encouraged to settle in Texas. Crude but tough, the Americans could create a buffer state between the barbarous tribes and north Mexico. They would let the *norteamericanos* fight the raiders, while south of the Rio Grande the Mexican states of Chihuahua, Coahuila, and Tamaulipas would prosper.

In 1821, impresario Steven F. Austin was given a massive land grant to bring Americans to settle. The Spaniards required only that the immigrants should accept the Catholic religion and swear allegiance to Spain. Within a few years, thousands of Americans had swarmed into the new lands, and when Mexico gained its independence in 1824, the new government allowed this influx to continue.

In 1830, a government survey determined that in Texas the *Anglos* outnumbered the Mexicans by four to one and the disparity was rapidly increasing. Fearing a loss of control, in April 1830, the Mexican government ended immigration and placed a heavy taxation on imports and exports in Texas. The near-bankrupt government in Mexico City also observed the growing export trade in cotton, beef, and other commodities, and saw in Texas a new source of revenue, so they sent soldiers and customs officials to the burgeoning Texas ports to collect taxes on all exports.

Texan and American ship owners, who had created the trade but had no voice in

Guerrillas armed with lances, *escopetas*, swords, and lassos fought ferociously in the many revolts that plagued Mexico. *(Gerry Embleton)*

the government, quickly asserted their right to smuggle. Soon their schooners sailed past Mexican customhouses, sometimes exchanging gunfire, and the increasing friction led to bloody skirmishes between Texan militia and Mexican regulars.

In an effort to redress grievances, Texas settlers called a convention and chose Stephen F. Austin to travel to Mexico City with proposals that they hoped would end the conflicts. After long wrangling with the Mexican government, Austin was imprisoned for treason. After two years in confinement he was released, on Christmas Day 1834, and returned to Texas.

Santa Anna, now dictator of Mexico, abrogated the liberal Mexican constitution of 1824 and ordered that all Texans be disarmed. The Texans refused to give up their weapons and clashes again broke out between the Anglo settlers and the Mexican soldiers.

In 1836, Santa Anna determined to establish control over the rebellious colony. At the head of an army he crossed the Rio Grande and invaded Texas. He overran the defenses of the old Alamo mission in San Antonio and slaughtered the few wounded survivors. On his orders a band of more than 300 rebels who had surrendered at the town of Goliad were summarily shot.

On 2 March 1836, the Texans, having assembled in convention, issued a declaration of independence, severing their ties with Mexico and declaring themselves an independent republic. On 20 April 1836, a furious and shrieking Texan army destroyed Santa Anna's forces at the battle of San Jacinto.

When captured, in order to save his neck from a hangman's noose, Santa Anna signed the Treaty of Velasco, granting Texas independence. The Mexican government refused to recognize the treaty, however, drove Santa Anna into exile, and maintained that Texas was still a province of Mexico.

In the decade that followed there were several ill-conceived Texan forays into Mexican territory. Twice, in March and September 1842, Mexican troops responded by invading Texas, raiding Gulf Coast towns, and capturing and looting San Antonio. There they arrested the city's leading citizens, marched them into Mexico, and flung them into the dreaded Perote prison.

From 1836 until 1843, Mexican warships attempted to blockade Texas ports and strangle the young republic's commerce. Texas retaliated by commissioning privateers. Later, they created a regular navy which wrecked Mexican seaborne trade, aided revolutionists in the Yucatán, and on occasion held Mexican Gulf Coast ports for ransom.

In May 1843, the sail-driven Texan flotilla fought two sea battles against a steam-driven Mexican fleet off the port of Campeche in the Yucatán. The main strength of the Mexican fleet lay in two modern British-built steamers manned by officers of the Royal Navy on long-term leave. Many of the gunners and engine mechanics were hired British Navy veterans. When the two forces collided, it marked the first battle between sail-driven and steam-driven warships. Tactically the battles were indecisive, although the Texans had few casualties while the Mexicans suffered many dead and wounded. Like Jutland in 1916, albeit on a much smaller scale, this encounter proved to be a massive strategic victory for Texas. The Mexican fleet never again attempted to blockade the Texas coast or launch a seaborne invasion from Matamoros or Vera Cruz.

During this decade of intermittent fighting, American public opinion sided with their former countrymen and exacerbated the increasing hostility between the two countries. As tensions mounted, many

Mexicans believed that the Americans were looking for a pretext to declare war. They cited as evidence a blundering American naval action in October 1842. Commodore Thomas Catesby Jones was anchored off a Peruvian port when he received news that war had broken out between the United States and Mexico. Without waiting for confirmation, he raised anchor and bent on all sail for California. Arriving off the port of Monterey on 20 October, he decided on bold and swift action. He sailed his squadron into the bay, anchored, and sent ashore an armed party of sailors and marines.

Marching to the town square, Jones read a proclamation announcing that he had captured the city for the United States. He ordered his troops to occupy the public buildings, had the Mexican flag hauled down, and raised the Stars and Stripes to the top of the square's flagpole. The Mexicans, more confused than alarmed, offered no resistance. Jones, satisfied with his coup, was gratified to see Thomas O. Larkin, the American consul at Monterey, approaching with a bewildered expression. After a brief exchange, expletives not recorded, Larkin informed him that there was no war. The United States was at peace with Mexico.

Blushing, Jones had the American flag hauled down and ordered that the Mexican flag be raised once more. He commanded his men to fire a musket salute as the Mexican tricolor again fluttered in the breeze, then proffered a profound apology to an apoplectic Mexican governor who, to say the least, was not amused.

Then Jones formed up his invading force and marched back to the wharf, where he and his men were rowed back to their ships. An embarrassed American government relieved Jones of command and sent him on a long voyage back to the United States. If tensions had not been so high, the affair might well have been laughed off. It was not. To many Mexicans the incident was an ominous portent of things to come and they were to be proved correct.

Meanwhile, American settlers had begun slipping into northern California and settling there illegally. In 1843, Santa Anna, ordered all Americans to leave California and Mexico's other western territories. This decree effectively throttled the lucrative trade between Sante Fe and St. Louis, which further antagonized American business interests.

The growing pressure from American expansionist politicians to annex Texas was alarming Mexicans. Early in 1845, when outgoing President John Tyler signed a joint resolution by Congress to make Texas part of the American union, Mexico severed diplomatic relations. A Mexican diplomatic note warned Tyler that annexation of Texas 'would be equivalent to a declaration of war against the Mexican Republic.'

Great Britain and France, both interested in gaining an economic foothold in the Texas Republic, attempted to foil annexation with the American Union. The British chargé d'affaires in Austin, Captain Charles Elliot, proposed a compromise to the two antagonistic countries. He told the Texan president, Anson Jones, that if he concluded a treaty with Mexico pledging that Texas would never annex itself to the United States, Britain and France would pressure the Mexican government to recognize Texas' independence. The Texan government, virtually bankrupt and tired of all the hostilities, rejected the proposal and pursued a policy seeking security in annexation.

In February 1845, James K. Polk was inaugurated as president. Physically frail but strong in purpose, Polk presided over a nation that was bursting at the seams. Immigrants were pouring into the country from Europe, and Americans were streaming west by the thousand, to lands claimed either by the Mexicans or, in the case of Oregon, by the British.

Pressure from businessmen and landless farmers demanded that the western territories be either purchased or taken by force. There were, however, obstacles. Russia was probing the west coast of North America with the intention of expanding its Alaskan possessions, but the British posed the major threat to American ambitions, with a dispute over the boundaries of the Oregon Territory that threatened conflict.

In November 1845, Polk sent John M. Slidell to Mexico City with an offer to buy all Mexican lands from the Texas border to the Pacific Ocean. He offered $25,000,000. As part of the deal, the American government would also pay to American citizens the claims they held against Mexico.

The Americans considered this offer to be more than fair. After all, Texas had maintained its independence for a decade and the other western lands were mostly vacant except for scattered Indian tribes and American squatters. Furthermore, the Americans claimed that these lands were only nominally held by Mexico, whose government was unable to exercise any authority over them.

Another cause of contention between the two countries were the claims Americans had against the Mexican government. These involved incidents of arbitrary seizure of American ships in Mexican ports, confiscation of American goods by corrupt customs officials, unjust imprisonment of American citizens, and the murders of other Americans. A mediation of the claims had been heard in a Prussian court in 1838, at which time the American claimants had been awarded millions of dollars. But Mexico was bankrupt, with an unstable government which within the first quarter century of independence had seen more than 30 different political administrations. Not surprisingly, after a few payments, Mexico defaulted on the bulk of the claims. To Mexicans, their penury was a further humiliation, and they allowed their pride to cloud their judgment of potential American military strength.

The Mexican government therefore refused to negotiate with Slidell and officially ignored his presence. They became hostile when, on 29 December 1845, Texas was admitted as the 28th state in the American union and became the 15th state to legalize slavery.

The slave states now held a majority of votes in the United States Senate.

American envoy John Slidell's attempts to purchase Mexican land were ignored by the government in Mexico City. (Ann Ronan Picture Library)

Abolitionists in New England feared a vast conspiracy was under way by the Southerners to forever dominate the government.

The Mexicans, enraged at the annexation of Texas, threatened war. Many blamed the United States for their debacle in Texas. One prominent newspaper declared the Americans to be the true enemy of Mexico and that they had secretly supported the Texan revolution while hiding behind an 'evil mask of hypocrisy.'

As war fever grew, some Mexicans harbored illusions that in the event of hostilities the American northern and eastern states would secede from the Union and would send arms and ammunition to support revolting Southern Negro slaves. The resulting chaos would enable Mexico to handily defeat the American armies.

The crisis over Oregon also gave Mexico a false sense of confidence: if war broke out,

Great Britain, with its mighty fleet and battle-tested army, would be their ally. Unknown to them, the British Foreign Office had agreed to negotiate the Oregon boundary dispute with the Americans. To Polk's relief, the threat of a two-front war with the British in the north and the Mexicans in the south had ended.

Some Mexicans, perhaps blinded by national pride, felt confident that their army, more than 20,000 strong, was well enough equipped and trained to easily defeat the 7,000 American regulars who were scattered in small posts along the western frontier. This, perhaps, was the most fateful illusion of all. The issues between the two neighbors might have been solved peacefully if more reason and less passion had prevailed, but Mexican intransigence and American aggressiveness combined to make war inevitable.

Courage the only common trait

The cultural differences between Americans and Mexicans carried over into both their political leaders and their armed forces.

The leaders

James Knox Polk, born on a farm in North Carolina in 1795, was sickly as a child and frail as a man, but he had a tireless energy in pursuing his expansionist policies. He graduated from the University of North Carolina at the top of his class, then studied law in Tennessee.

Polk soon found a mentor in Andrew Jackson, and followed the Jackson philosophy of championing the cause of the common man, as opposed to the Virginia aristocrats and the New England Brahmins. He was elected to the Tennessee legislature and later became governor of Tennessee. In November 1844, Polk secured the Democratic Party nomination for the presidency and was elected on a platform of westward expansion.

Major General Winfield Scott, 60 years old in 1846, was the most experienced and capable officer in the American army. At age 28 he had been a brigadier general during the war of 1812. Although egotistical and pompous, he was an excellent tactician and a shrewd strategist with a gift for going for the jugular.

Zachary Taylor, 62 years old, was an experienced frontier soldier. The opposite of Scott in dress and manners, he was loved by his men for his lack of formality. An indifferent tactician, his bold aggressiveness and determination were the keys to his victories. His military reputation later led him to the American presidency.

The dominant leader of Mexico for more than 20 years was Antonio Lopez de Santa Anna. President, dictator, and commander of the Mexican armies, his reputation among the Mexican people seesawed between great hero and great villain. Although devious and corrupt, on occasion he could rouse the Mexicans to extreme bravery and endurance.

General Pedro de Ampudia, one-time commander of the Army of the North, had a reputation based more on cruelty than on military ability. Once, when revolting soldiers had surrendered to him with a promise of clemency, he had had them shot, then cut off their leader's head, boiled it in oil, and hung it on a pike in the main square of San Juan Bautista.

General Mariano Arista was perhaps more of a gentleman, and too much of a

President James K. Polk was elected by vowing to acquire the Oregon Territory, annex Texas, and purchase California. (Ann Ronan Picture Library)

politician, to be a successful leader in battle. Following early failures, he was relieved of command. After the war, he became president of Mexico for a short while.

If American campaigns were won by generals, during the war with Mexico, battles were won through the excellence of junior officers, and if there was one determinant factor in American successes, it was the United States Military Academy at West Point, in New York State. The discipline and training delivered there, particularly in engineering and in the use of light artillery, turned the tide of many of the fiercest battles of the war. Among its graduates was Robert E. Lee, arguably the most gifted commander in all of America's wars. It was his personal reconnaissance work that made great contributions to American victories at Buena Vista, Vera Cruz, and Scott's successful campaign on the road to Mexico City. In later years, Lee led the armies of the Confederate States of America.

Ulysses S. Grant, who became the commander in chief of the Union armies during the American Civil War and later a president of the United States, was a successful and innovative subaltern, often cited for bravery.

Jefferson Davis, also a West Pointer, returned to the army to lead the fabled 1st Mississippi Volunteer Regiment, which had a key role in turning the tide of battle at Buena Vista. He later became president of the Confederate States of America.

Thomas 'Stonewall' Jackson served as an artillery officer, one of those young West Pointers who employed the tactical mobility and accurate gunnery that proved decisive on the battlefield.

Mexican officers, on the other hand, though always brave and often competent, were mainly aristocrats who had little rapport with common soldiers and were often contemptuous of them. While

Antonio Lopez de Santa Anna was the devious, sometime dictator, of Mexico. He gave away Texas after his defeat at San Jacinto but rallied the Mexican people against the American invasion. (AKG Berlin)

graduates from the Mexican military academy were knowledgeable professionals, many other officers were political appointees whose resplendent uniforms belied their lack of military expertise.

Trained in Spanish military tradition and tactics, the officer corps was, nevertheless, cursed with competing political philosophies. They were royalists or rebels against Spain, federalists who believed in the primacy of local self-government, and centralists who wished for a strong, all-controlling government in Mexico City. Some of them had fought against each other during the many political upheavals and revolts that plagued Mexico. Indeed, these internal splits often disrupted what should have been a common cause against an alien invader.

General Winfield Scott was nicknamed 'Old Fuss and Feathers' for his love of pomp and ceremony. He was a competent tactician and a shrewd strategist. It was Scott's plan to launch a seaborne attack and then march on the Mexican capital. (Library of Congress)

The soldiers

The differences between the enlisted ranks of both armies were even greater. Some of the

American enlisted men in the regular army joined for adventure, but for most it was economic necessity. The $7.00 per month, three square meals a day, and warm clothes were an inducement to many immigrants who wanted to learn the language or inculcate themselves into American life. One estimate puts more than two-thirds of the enlistees as foreign born. The majority were Irish, but there were also large contingents of Germans and British.

The regulars, though few in number, were well drilled and were led by officers experienced in frontier fighting and trained to the exacting standards of West Point. A

In the American armies, the regulars were drilled like European troops. The volunteers were indifferent to military etiquette but prided themselves as tough fighting men. (Library of Congress)

major failing of the peacetime army was the harsh discipline – the lash was not unknown. A favorite punishment was 'bucking and gagging,' in which a miscreant, hands and feet tied, had a stick pushed under his knees and over his elbows, locking his arms and legs together. Then a tent peg or stick was forced between his teeth and tied in place. Left for hours, he suffered pain, thirst and humiliation. These severe punishments and the arrogance of some officers were major causes for desertion, especially among the Irish.

The volunteers were different. When the war broke out, young men by the tens of thousands, mostly from the southern and western states, swamped recruiting stations. Many had to be turned away for lack of uniforms and equipment, but what the volunteer regiments lacked in experience

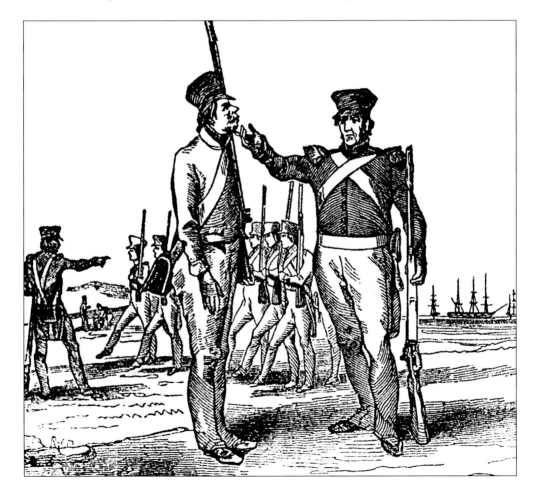

VOLUNTEERS !

Men of the Granite State!

Men of Old Rockingham!! the

strawberry-bed of patriotism, renowned for bravery and devotion to Country, rally at this call. Santa Anna, reeking with the generous confidence and magnanimity of your countrymen, is in arms, eager to plunge his traitor-dagger in their bosoms. To arms, then, and rush to the standard of the fearless and gallant CUSHING----put to the blush the dastardly meanness and rank toryism of Massachusetts. Let the half civilized Mexicans hear the crack of the unerring New Hampshire rifleman, and illustrate on the plains of San Luis Potosi, the fierce, determined, and undaunted bravery that has always characterized her sons.

Col. THEODORE F. ROWE, at No. 31 Daniel-street, is authorized and will enlist men this week for the Massachusetts Regiment of Volunteers. The compensation is $10 per month---$30 in advance. Congress will grant a handsome bounty in money and ONE HUNDRED AND SIXTY ACRES OF LAND.

Portsmouth, Feb. 2. 1847.

This jingoistic recruiting poster appealed to the American chauvinistic spirit, but most of New England was bitterly opposed to the war, fearing that its spoils would extend slavery into the west. (Library of Congress)

Although the best scouts and antiguerrilla fighters in the army, the Texas Rangers were also wild, vengeful men. But on occasion they could play as hard and as unruly as they fought. (Archives Division, Texas State Library)

and training they made up for in enthusiasm and dedication. They elected their officers, and if military courtesy and expertise were lacking among them, leadership in battle was not. Mostly young men in their late teens or early twenties, they learned quickly.

An early disadvantage of the volunteer system was that they were obligated to serve only 12 months. After many battle-hardened regiments chose to return at the expiration of their service, regulations were changed to hold volunteers until the end of hostilities.

To the consternation of regular officers, the volunteers considered themselves more as citizens than soldiers and regarded the strict hierarchy of the regulars as demeaning and silly. Volunteer officers learned to control their men with a loose rein.

Some volunteer regiments had their fighting record marred by lack of discipline, rowdy behavior, looting, and, not uncommonly, crimes against the Mexican civilian population. The Texans were the worst.

The enlisted ranks of the Mexican army were mostly made up of peasant conscripts, selected by lot for a six-year tour of duty. Bachelors and married men without children from 18 to 40 years of age were required to serve. Middle-class men with political connections could usually gain an exemption if they did not wish to be officers.

Unlike the robust Americans, most of whom were farmers raised on a diet of fresh meat, wheat bread, and vegetables, the Mexican soldier was often less than five feet two inches tall and was poorly fed on a diet of Indian corn, rice, and beans. Compounding the confusion of inadequate training, most of the peasant soldiers were illiterate; many spoke and understood only the Indian dialects of their tribe.

If the Americans could be combative over military discipline, the Mexican soldier simply deserted. A most unfunny joke in that army was the not always apocryphal story of the Mexican line officer writing to a military depot: 'I am returning your shackles. Please send me more volunteers.'

If the men of these armies had anything in common, it was that officers and enlisted men alike almost always showed uncommon courage under fire.

The navies

Throughout the war, the ships of the United States Navy controlled the Atlantic and Pacific coastlines of Mexico. They blockaded Mexican ports, landed marines in support of army troops and irregulars on the California coastline, transported Scott's army to Vera Cruz, helped smash enemy defenses at that port with naval gunfire, and supplied weaponry, ammunition, rations, and reinforcements to the 10,000 American troops in Scott's expeditionary force.

The nearest United States naval base was at Pensacola, Florida, 900 miles from Vera Cruz. The American blockading force suffered constantly from a lack of coal and fresh food, from outbreaks of yellow fever, inadequate coastal charts and violent storms that struck suddenly during summer and winter months. However, with a mixture of

sail and steam ships, the Navy, even under these difficult circumstances, was a determining factor in the American victory.

The Mexican Navy was unable to protect their merchant fleet or break the American blockade and was plagued by lack of funds, a shortage of spare parts, and an indifferent government. Worst of all, they lacked competent officers and crews. At the outbreak

These Mexican dragoons were great horsemen and experienced fighters, having served through incessant rebellions. They and their officers were brave and bold, sometimes to the point of folly. (Library of Congress)

of hostilities, they sold, scuttled, or burned most of their ships rather than fight a superior American force. Consequently, the Mexican Navy played no significant part in the war.

Opening guns

Following his inauguration in March 1845, President Polk took action to protect the country's new southern border. He ordered General Zachary Taylor, then commanding troops in Louisiana, to move his force to Texas and be prepared to march into the disputed area south of the Nueces River.

In July, Taylor and 3,500 men, almost half of the entire United States regular army, were encamped near the coastal town of Corpus Christi. In February 1846, Taylor received orders to proceed to Port Isabel, near the mouth of the Rio Grande River. Establishing his supply base at Port Isabel, Taylor then marched his men 30 miles south-west to the north bank of the Rio Grande. There his men constructed a fortified position named Fort Texas, from which his artillery could command the town of Matamoros on the opposite bank. The Americans now confronted a Mexican force of 6,000 men on the south bank. This was the Army of the North, under the command of the notorious General Pedro de Ampudia.

On 12 April, Ampudia sent a message to Taylor declaring that the Americans were camped on Mexican territory. He demanded they withdraw to the Nueces or 'arms and arms alone will decide this question.' Taylor indignantly refused and both armies prepared to fight. On 24 April, the explosive Ampudia was replaced by General Mariano Arista. For a few days calm prevailed.

In the meantime, John Slidell, who had lingered in Mexico City from November 1845 until March 1846, vainly attempting to open negotiations with the Mexican government, gave up and returned to the United States. President Polk complained to Congress that the Mexicans had 'refused to receive him or listen to his propositions.' Polk then sent instructions to Commander John D. Sloat's command in Pacific waters. If war broke out, Sloat was to seize and occupy California's principal ports.

Commander David Connor, leading the United States Navy Home Squadron operating in the Gulf of Mexico, was ordered to be prepared to blockade the eastern coast of Mexico, protect American commerce from privateers, and assist army operations. To patrol the hundreds of miles of Mexican coast, Connor would have two

General Mariano Arista wrote Taylor that the troops under his command 'will exhibit the feelings of humanity and generosity which are genial to them.' They were perhaps too genial, and after Arista lost the battles of Palo Alto and Resaca de la Palma, he was relieved of command. (Archives Division, Texas State Library)

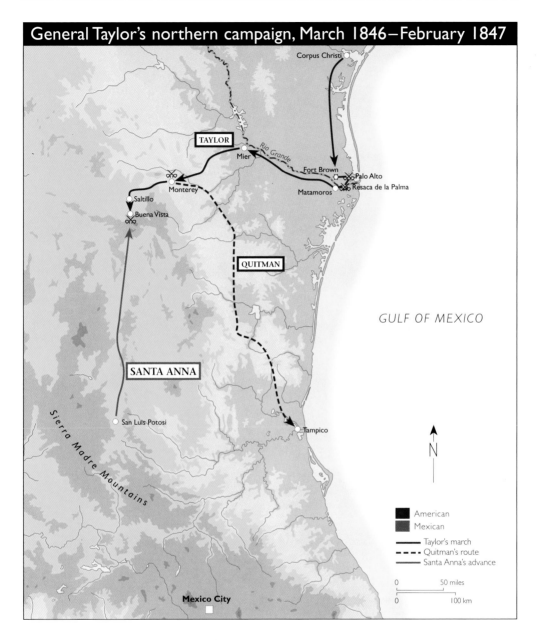

General Taylor's northern campaign, March 1846–February 1847

Corpus Christi

TAYLOR

Mier

Rio Grande

Fort Brown

Palo Alto

Monterey

Resaca de la Palma

Matamoros

Saltillo

Buena Vista

QUITMAN

GULF OF MEXICO

SANTA ANNA

Sierra Madre Mountains

San Luis Potosi

Tampico

N

■ American
■ Mexican
—— Taylor's march
- - - Quitman's route
—— Santa Anna's advance

0   50 miles
0   100 km

Mexico City

powerful steamers, *Mississippi* and *Princeton*, two big frigates, three sloops, five brigs, and a schooner.

Santa Anna had regained the presidency in 1843. As with his previous administrations, he led Mexico into bankruptcy and revolt. In revulsion, his political opponents seized power and Santa Anna was captured and thrown into Perote prison until May 1845, when he was exiled for life and deported to Cuba.

Winning battles at Palo Alto and Resaca de Palma in early May 1846, Taylor crossed the Rio Grande at the head of 6,000 men. Marching west, parallel with the river, he reached Mier, then swung his army south-west onto the Monterey Road. Slowed by logistical problems and the boiling heat of the northern Mexico summer, he reached Monterey on 21 September. After smashing the Mexican army and capturing the city, he arranged a truce. Then he took up defensive positions in the mountains south of Saltillo. Later in the war, a detachment of Taylor's troops occupied Tampico. In February 1847, General Santa Anna, in power once more, led an army north from San Luis Potosi hoping to crush the Americans and regain control of the north.

On 14 April 1846, Arista informed Taylor
that hostilities had commenced. Shortly
afterwards, a Mexican force clashed with a
troop of dragoons north of the Rio Grande,
killing or wounding 16 Americans.

The Mexican government threatened war if the United
States annexed Texas. After annexation, President Polk
sent General Zachary Taylor and an army to Corpus
Christi with orders to march to the Rio Grande River, the
new boundary of the United States. (Library of Congress)

On 30 April, the Mexican commander
crossed the Rio Grande with 4,000 men,
hoping to interpose his forces between
Taylor's army at Fort Texas and the
American supply base at Port Isabel.

When Texan scouts reported the Mexican
move, 'Old Rough and Ready' Taylor left a
small force to hold Fort Texas and ordered
the bulk of his men on a forced march to
Port Isabel. After 20 hours of slogging the
30 miles to the port, Taylor ordered his

exhausted men to throw up a defensive line around the town.

The situation changed when Arista ordered Ampudia to attack Fort Texas. After a Texas Ranger slipped through the Mexican lines to report the siege of the American fort, Taylor decided to take the offensive. Although outnumbered almost three to one, on 7 May, Taylor's 2,200-man army marched south on the Matamoros Road to relieve Fort Texas.

Arista took up a strong defensive position across the road, along a ridge called Palo Alto. He ordered Ampudia to abandon the siege of Fort Texas and join his command. Arista deployed 6,000 men in a mile-long frontage and awaited the American attack. He placed part of his cavalry by a swamp to guard his left flank and another detachment of mounted troops on a wooded hill protecting his right. He spread his infantry, interspersed with artillery batteries, in the center, across the road.

On the hot, muggy morning of 8 May, Taylor's sweat-soaked men stomped along the sandy road until they came to a halt one mile from the enemy. Taylor, wearing his customary baggy blue jeans, a stained white duster, and a battered straw hat, looked more like a down-on-his-luck farmer than a commanding general. Sitting sidewise on his horse and occasionally spitting an amber stream of tobacco juice, Taylor calmly deployed his men. With the exception of the mounted Texas Rangers, they were all regulars.

Taylor's immediate concern was his supply train – 300 cumbersome wagons being hauled by a motley assortment of mules and oxen. To protect them from a lightning attack by Mexican cavalry, he reluctantly diverted a battery of artillery and a squadron of dragoons.

Taylor placed his large 18-pounder guns in the center of the road and moved his troops to form a line of skirmishers. He placed the 8th Infantry Regiment on his far left flank, supported by Captain James Duncan's light artillery battery. In the center, straddling the 18-pounders, he deployed the 3rd and 4th Infantry Regiments. To their right he placed Major Samuel Ringgold and his battery, supporting the 5th Infantry Regiment on the extreme right flank.

Ringgold, like many young West Point graduate artillerists, was eager to test his new Flying Artillery, lightweight, horse drawn-guns designed to be deployed and fired rapidly. He had been a pioneer in

their development from 1838 and had
designed the high-wheeled, light caisson
which enabled the bronze 6-pounder guns
to be maneuvered across rugged terrain at
great speed. He had also written the
manual, *Instruction for Field Artillery,
Horse and Foot*, which was used in the
rigorous training given to officers and men

On 8 May 1846, the first major battle between the
Mexican and American armies was fought on the coastal
plain of Palo Alto. On the first day of battle, American
artillery beat off Mexican assaults. The following day,
American infantrymen cracked the Mexico lines and sent
them into retreat. President Polk told Congress:
'American blood has been shed on American soil' and
the war was on. (Painting by Carl Nebel, Archives
Division, Texas State Library)

in that branch of the service. These light
batteries were the cream of the army,
and Taylor had three of them, each with
four guns.

The 6-pounders weighed only 880lbs and
had a range of 1,500 yards, which enabled
the artillery to remain out of the range of
enemy musketry when necessary. The guns
could fire solid shot, explosive shells, and
canister (a metal can filled with musket balls
which when fired sprayed the balls, turning
the cannon into a kind of large shotgun).
American tactical doctrine called for the
Flying Artillery to be placed on the firing
line at the point of the greatest danger.

At 2.00pm on 8 May, as the Americans
formed into line, the Mexican artillery

bloody tangle of dying horses and men. Tragically, Major Ringgold was killed by one of the few accurate cannonballs fired by the Mexican gunners.

Arista then ordered his remaining cavalry to flank the American left and destroy the American wagon park. They met with equally devastating artillery fire from Duncan's battery and quickly withdrew to their lines. The constant firing set the prairie grass afire and soon oily black smoke enveloped the battlefield. Under this cover, Arista ordered a withdrawal. As the Mexicans retreated, they could hear the screams of their wounded, burning to death in the flaming grass.

Resaca de la Palma

After the smoke cleared and the casualties were counted, the American losses were half a dozen killed and 40 wounded. Mexican casualties were estimated at between 400 and 700.

Arista moved his demoralized troops to a point above Matamoros, on the north bank of the Rio Grande, and deployed them along a sunken dried-up river bed called Resaca de la Palma. His position was further protected by thorn bushes, thick cactus, and swampy ground. He placed his infantry in the stream bed, with his artillery behind them; the cavalry was held in reserve in the rear. Confident that this position could not be taken, Arista retired to his headquarters tent far behind his lines to write dispatches.

The following morning, 9 May, Taylor ordered an advance. Seeking a double envelopment of the Mexican flanks, he sent infantry through the rough country on both sides of the road. Fighting their way through the almost impassable thorns and brush, which ripped their uniforms and tore at their flesh, they made little progress. When finally they reached both sides of the ravine, they attacked with bayonets and clubbed their enemies with rifle butts.

began firing at extreme range. Without explosive shells, they fired solid cannonballs which after a few hundred yards began bouncing over the rough ground, losing velocity.

The quick-firing American guns got off eight shots to the Mexicans' one and Arista's infantry began to falter. The Mexican general countered by ordering his magnificently uniformed lancers to attack the American right flank. With pennons fluttering from their lance heads and buglers sounding the charge, they galloped into disaster. Ringgold's battery, each gun firing one round a minute, blasted them with explosive shells and then decimated their ranks with canister. Soon the field was a

Major Samuel Ringgold was mortally wounded by a
Mexican cannonball while directing his artillery battery
during the first day's fighting at Palo Alto. The projectile
drove through his right thigh, passed through his horse,
and ripped into his left leg. (Library of Congress)

When the attack on the Mexican left
was repulsed by a Mexican battery firing from
the roadway, Taylor ordered Major Charles
May's squadron of the 2nd Dragoons to charge
down the Matamoros Road and silence the
enemy guns. In a column of fours, sabers
flashing, the Americans charged at the gallop.
They overran the guns but found themselves
surrounded by enraged infantrymen slashing
at their mounts with bayonets. May ordered

his bugler to blow recall and, turning about,
they galloped back to the American lines.

Taylor, exercising his fluent frontier
vocabulary, sent the 8th Infantry down the
road to take and 'this time to keep the guns.'
The headlong charge of the 8th broke the
Mexican lines and they took possession of
the battery. The American infantry had by
then enveloped both flanks, and some units
had reached the Matamoros Road, cutting off
the Mexican line of retreat. Demoralized,
Arista's troops panicked. Some surrendered
while others scattered and ran for the river.
More than 300 drowned or were picked off
like grounded ducks by American infantry as
they tried to reach the south bank.

Estimates put Mexican losses at more than 1,200 killed or wounded, 100 captured, and 2,000 deserted. For days the skies were filled with gorged vultures, while howling wolves roamed the battlefield feasting on the unburied dead. American losses were put at 34 killed and 113 wounded.

On 11 May, a truce was agreed upon and on 17 May, the survivors of the Army of the North evacuated Matamoros and straggled south. Taylor's army crossed the river and occupied the town. For a while northern Mexico would be quiet.

When President Polk learned of the first skirmish he sent a war message to Congress asking for 50,000 volunteers and ordered Mexican ports blockaded.

War across the continent

As each side mobilized, the inevitable confusion and shortages stalled major offensives by both armies for months. While preparing for battle, the vast differences between the American and Mexican forces became increasingly apparent.

The Americans

The declaration of war passed by the American Congress approved the expenditure of 10 million dollars and authorized 50,000 volunteers, to be raised by the states, to carry the burden of the fighting. Within days, volunteers flocked to the recruiting depots. Most were spurred by patriotism and a lust for adventure, but generous land grants for veterans also helped recruiting.

The flintlock musket, weighing 10lbs and firing a .68 caliber lead ball, was standard equipment for the United States infantry. A few units, however, had rifles adapted for the new, more efficient, percussion caps. Battle sights were set for approximately 120 yards, but the weapon could be effective up to 200 yards.

A cartridge known as 'buck and ball' was also issued. Consisting of one normal-sized ball and three smaller ones, it was lethal when fired at close range. Troops were expected to fire three aimed rounds per minute, and were drilled until the loading and firing sequences became a reflex action.

Several units, including the Mounted Rifles Regiment and the 1st Mississippi Volunteers, were armed with rifles that had an effective range of more than 400 yards in the hands of a trained regular or a frontier marksman. Rifles were slow to reload because the ball had to be rammed down the barrel. At best, it took one full minute per shot. Most of the shoulder weapons had attachments for bayonets.

The two dragoon regiments were outfitted with shortened carbine versions of the infantry musket and usually used percussion caps. For the charge, they wielded sabers and fired a single-shot percussion cap pistol. The Texas Rangers, arguably the most deadly mounted troops in the war, carried one and often two of the new Colt 5-shot repeating pistols.

The regular army wore uniforms of blue wool, while the volunteers at first sported a variety of colors and styles. As the war progressed, volunteers were provided with more regulation attire by army quartermasters. As the armies marched deeper into Mexico, shoes, pants, and shirts became difficult to replace and soon the columns resembled bands of wandering hoboes.

The provision of food was always a problem. Rations shipped from New Orleans depots were often spoiled and uneatable when they arrived in camp. One soldier test for meat was to throw it against a wall. If it stuck, it was best not to eat it.

Regulations provided for ample amounts of meat, bread, vegetables, coffee, salt, and sugar, but it was rare that such a variety was available. Fortunately, Mexicans were happy to sell local foodstuffs to Americans in exchange for cash in the form of silver or gold coins. Their food was better and cost less than that offered by sutlers, who were damned for their high prices and poor merchandise. The Americans soon acquired a taste for Mexican dishes, and tamales, enchiladas, tacos, and tortillas rated higher in soldiers' tastes than did salt beef and stale bread.

While in camp, the men gathered around mess fires to socialize, play interminable card games, gripe about the food, and dream about the women they had left behind. The more educated held literary readings, produced comical plays, or held debates on the issues of the day. Sing-alongs were popular for all – *Home Sweet Home* and *The Girl I Left Behind Me* were favorites. Near towns, however, where hard liquor was available, merriment often degenerated into brawls. In the city bordellos, gonorrhea and syphilis were endemic.

Like most 19th century wars, more men were lost to disease than were killed in battle. Spoiled food, contaminated water, and unsanitary disposal of human and animal wastes caused most of the problems. A lack of tents resulted in soldiers sleeping on the ground in mud and water, exposed to wind, rain, sandstorms, and cold. These conditions often resulted in lethal cases of pneumonia. Long marches in the sometimes boiling Mexican sun were a not uncommon killer for men loaded with a 10-pound rifle, 40 rounds of ammunition, bayonet, blanket, water jug, rations, and cooking gear. The roads from St. Louis to California, Vera Cruz to Mexico City, and the Rio Grande to Buena Vista all took their toll of American dead.

Unskilled doctors and nurses, poor facilities and equipment, and the general ignorance of the medical profession provided little help to men stricken by exhaustion, illness, or battle wounds, and the death toll was extremely high.

The Mexicans

Mexico was handicapped by a lack of factories to produce arms and ammunition, and after the outbreak of the war, the American blockade choked off European sources of weapons.

Mexican fusiliers and grenadiers were issued the British-made Brown Bess musket, a smooth-bore flintlock firing a .75 caliber lead ball. Riflemen were issued British-made Baker flintlock rifles of .62 caliber, accurate up to 200 yards. Both weapons were equipped for bayonet use.

Mexican marksmanship was extremely poor. Conscripts rarely underwent the vigorous drilling needed for fast loading and accurate shooting, and the shortage of ammunition meant that some conscripts

only fired their weapons for the first time when engaged in battle.

Mexican-manufactured gunpowder was of poor quality, so extra gunpowder was loaded into each cartridge. The added kick when a trigger was pulled made the shooter flinch, often sending his bullet high or wide of its mark.

Cavalry was the elite force in the Mexican army and was better equipped and uniformed than the infantry. The favorite weapon for mounted troops was the lance, a 12-foot wooden shaft topped with an iron spearhead. A red pennon attached at the end fluttered during a charge, designed to startle enemy horses. Cavalrymen were usually issued *escopetas*, a short-barreled flintlock carbine, a single-shot flintlock pistol, a long straight-bladed saber, and often a lasso.

Mexican artillery was often old and usually employed obsolescent tactics. Heavy barrels and caissons made their guns, ranging from 24-pounder siege guns to 8-pounder field guns, hard to maneuver and slow to deploy. Again, a shortage of gunpowder allowed little training, and a lack of modern explosive shells made their artillery less effective.

Elite units, usually cavalry, were often resplendent in brightly colored Napoleonic-era uniforms. Most of the army, however, was poorly dressed, with bright-colored tailcoats and rough canvas pants, white in summer and, if available, blue in winter. The peasant infantry marched in sandals or barefoot. There were shortages of tents, blankets, and overcoats.

The rank and file of the Mexican army was not only untrained, ill-clothed, and poorly equipped, but was also usually underfed. With an inefficient commissary, troops usually had to live off the land. Around the campfires there were cards, songs, and comradeship, dances and an occasional cock fight. Among the officers there were horse races and interminable political discussions. Many peasant soldiers, drafted and marched far from their native villages, suffered the same longings and homesickness as their American opponents. Poor clothing, lack of tents and

warm clothes, and inadequate diets reduced many sturdy peasant soldiers to invalids. With ailing and embittered soldiers, the Mexican army faced escalating desertion rates.

California

While northern Mexico was exploding in battle, California was boiling over with revolution. During June 1846, the illegal population of 1,000 Americans, who were tough trappers, deserters from whaling fleets, and gold hunters, revolted against Mexico.

The giant province of California was virtually uninhabited, with a total population of less than 10,000 of European ancestry. The settlers were centered around the ports of San Francisco, Monterey, Los Angeles, and San Diego. Isolated from

The Americans washed out filthy uniforms whenever time and clear water were available. But unsanitary conditions and disease were responsible for 11,000 deaths among the troops. (Library of Congress)

Mexico City by virtually impassible deserts and thousands of miles, California was ripe to be plucked by anyone with a few guns and much daring.

The Americans had the guns and in Captain John C. Fremont they found a leader of reckless courage. Fremont, who had led previous explorations into the west, was guided to Sutter's Fort by famed scout Kit Carson in December 1845. After war was declared he joined the Bear Flaggers and led them into a series of victorious skirmishes with Mexican forces. On 7 July 1846, he joined forces with the American naval flotilla and together, with little opposition, they

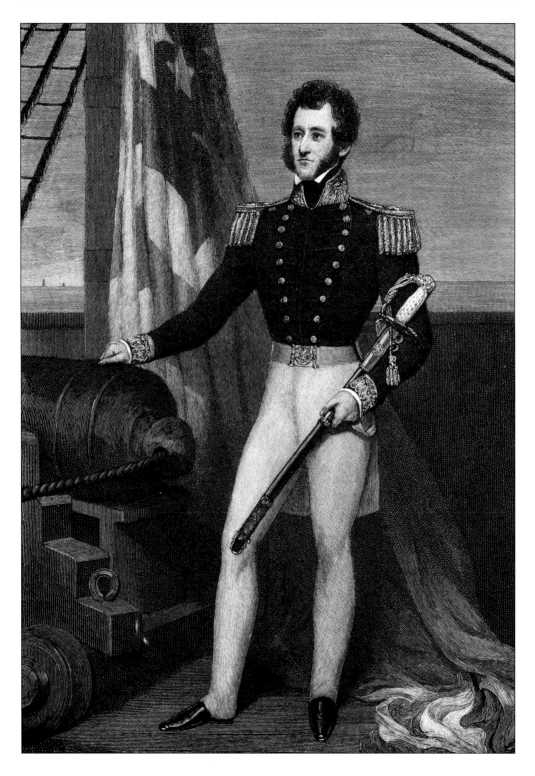

Commodore Robert F. Stockton commanded the American
flotilla off the coast of California. He sent landing parties to seize
ports from San Francisco to San Diego. (Corbis)

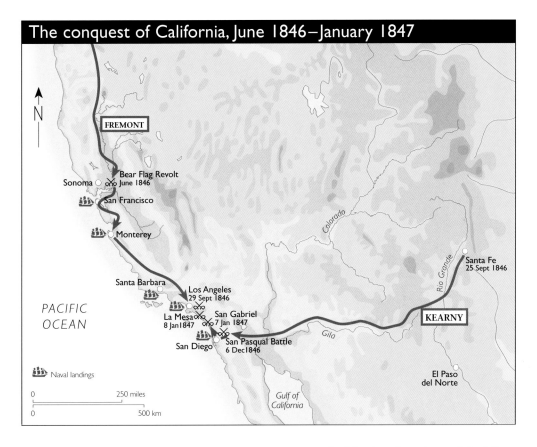

The conquest of California, June 1846–January 1847

N

FREMONT

Sonoma

Bear Flag Revolt
June 1846

San Francisco

Monterey

Colorado

Santa Fe
25 Sept 1846

Rio Grande

Santa Barbara

Los Angeles
29 Sept 1846

PACIFIC
OCEAN

La Mesa
8 Jan 1847

San Gabriel
7 Jan 1847

KEARNY

Gila

San Diego

San Pasqual Battle
6 Dec 1846

Naval landings

0   250 miles

0   500 km

El Paso
del Norte

*Gulf of
California*

In June 1846, hundreds of Americans who had settled illegally in California rose in revolt and declared independence. Aided by American John C. Fremont, illegally conducting a surveying expedition in the area, they seized San Francisco. The commander of a United States naval squadron in the area assumed the war with Mexico had started, and on 7 July, he sent landing parties to seize ports along the northern coast.

By mid-August the Navy, led by Commander Robert F. Stockton, had, in cooperation with the irregular soldiers of the 'Bear Flag Republic,' occupied Los Angeles and the remaining Californian ports.

Meanwhile Brigadier General Stephen W. Kearny, guided by scout Kit Carson, left Santa Fe on 25 September and arrived in California in early December. After several skirmishes, the Mexican forces were defeated and by the New Year the American flag flew uncontested over California.

occupied port cities from Los Angeles to San Diego. The American naval commander, Commodore Robert F. Stockton, appointed Fremont as Governor of California, an act that would lead to bitter rivalries.

In May 1846, a frontier soldier, Brigadier General Stephen Watts Kearny, was given

command of the American Army of the West and was ordered to capture Sante Fe, secure the New Mexico–Arizona area, and then march to California. The chief of staff of the American army, General Winfield Scott, awarded Kearny the title of Military Governor of New Mexico and California. Kearny thus had the honor of being the third simultaneous governor of the Pacific province, vying with Fremont and Mexican Governor Pio de Jesus Pico for control of California.

Kearny had pacified New Mexico by late September. Soon afterwards he and a small force of 100 dragoons began the long dry march across the desert to California. During the first week of December, after having traveled 1,000 miles from Fort Leavenworth, Kearny and his exhausted men staggered into California.

The brigadier soon learned that a force of Mexican lancers under the command of Andres Pico was planning to attack his tired force. Pico's men were camped near the small village of San Pascual. Although he knew he was outnumbered, Kearny determined to attack. At 2.00am on 6 December 1846, he led a stumbling advance through a ravine.

Kearny's column of dragoons, accompanied by 35 sailors and marines of Stockton's force who had joined him, and two small howitzers, edged to the end of the ravine and into the valley. At the first glimmerings of daylight, Kearny ordered the charge. Pico, however, had heard his approach and ordered his men to mount their horses with lances at the ready.

As Kearny's worn-out horses and mules limped to the attack, the center of Pico's line seemed to falter and the lancers wheeled about and ran from the Americans. Shouting 'Hurrah,' the American dragoons spurred their mounts and emboldened by the Mexican retreat charged in a strung-out and staggering line of pursuit. After retreating 100 yards, the fleeing Mexicans jerked to a stop, wheeled about, lowered their lances, and charged the straggling and surprised dragoons. The 150 lancers hit the Americans like a thunderbolt, killing 18 men almost instantly and wounding another 15, including Kearny, who took a lance point in the groin.

The Americans, with almost a third of their force dead or wounded, retreated to a nearby rocky hill. One of the howitzers, hauled by frightened mules, disappeared over the horizon and into the desert in a cloud of dust. Kearny was besieged for three days until a relief column of sailors and marines arrived and Pico retreated.

By the end of December, Kearny had joined forces with the naval contingents in San Diego. They marched and sailed north, defeating Mexican forces in battles at the San Gabriel River and La Mesa. By early January, they controlled California. In the new year the fighting also became political, when Kearny and Fremont each claimed dominance in California. Kearny won out, receiving a promotion to major general; Fremont, charged with insubordination, returned to Washington, D.C. in disgrace.

Doniphan's march

At the outbreak of the war, Alexander W. Doniphan, a six-foot-six, 240-pound Missouri lawyer, helped raise 1,000 men to form the 1st Regiment of Missouri Mounted Volunteers. In mid-August 1846, the regiment marched from Fort Leavenworth, Kansas, to join Kearny in Sante Fe. When Kearny headed for California, Doniphan turned south and marched into legend.

In December, headed for the Rio Grande and the city of El Paso del Norte, Doniphan's men traversed the desolate *Jornada del Muerto*, the feared Journey of Death, a sandy, rocky wasteland, bereft of water or foliage, with only dust storms and rattlesnakes to break the barren monotony of the 250-mile trek. On Christmas Day his parched men and horses stumbled to the welcome banks of the Rio Grande River and gulped its muddy waters. Suddenly, a scout on a foaming, lathered horse, galloped into camp shouting that hundreds of Mexican mounted troops and infantry were moving rapidly toward their camp. Bugles blared, and the Americans ran for their weapons and formed a line across the road to El Paso del Norte.

The Mexican commander ordered a halt 500 yards from the American camp and a Mexican dragoon officer, wearing a green jacket trimmed in scarlet, with brass-topped helmet gleaming in the sun, approached. He carried a black flag displaying two white skulls and crossed bones, and shouted: 'Surrender or we will charge.' Doniphan, through his interpreter was said to have replied: 'Charge and be damned.'

The Mexican wheeled his horse, shouted: 'We will give no quarter,' and rode back to a long line of deploying troops. Soon, with a blaring of bugles, more than 1,500 Mexican cavalrymen and infantrymen rushed the American line. The Mexicans paused at 400 yards and fired three volleys which roared over the heads of the crouching Missourians. Then they charged.

The Mexicans were 150 yards away when the Volunteers rose up and poured volley after volley into their ranks. More than

200 were killed or wounded before they turned and fled. Seven of Doniphan's men were slightly wounded. Two days later, the Missourians crossed the Rio Grande and took possession of El Paso del Norte without a shot being fired.

On 8 February, Doniphan and his small army, reinforced by 100 men and an artillery battery, marched south toward Ciudad Chihuahua. After crossing the arid country, always short of water, the Americans neared the Rio Sacramento, some 15 miles from the city. There, in late February, stretched across the road leading to the capital of the state of Chihuahua, were 3,000 Mexican soldiers with 10 artillery pieces.

Outnumbered three to one, Doniphan shied away from a frontal attack. He skirted the road to the west, maneuvered his men, guns, and wagons through a gulch, then drove them up a steep cliff and onto a mesa, outflanking the Mexican position.

As his artillery fire enfiladed the Mexican line, Doniphan dismounted some of his men and then charged the now disorganized foe. Gun butts smashed and Bowie knives slashed in close-quarter fighting until the Mexicans retreated in disorder. Doniphan reported that he had captured 10 guns and 10 wagons, killed 300, and wounded another 300. His losses were two killed and a few slightly wounded. One of the captured wagons was filled with lassos, which the Mexican general had planned to use to tie up his Missouri prisoners.

The Volunteers marched into Chihuahua on 1 March and Doniphan rested his men until late April; then he again marched south. On the way, his men ambushed a band of Lipan Indians who had ravished the women and murdered the men at a ranch near Parras. Freeing the women captives, the Missourians continued their trek, swinging eastward to join Taylor's army at Buena Vista.

From there they hiked to Matamoros, boarded ship, and sailed to New Orleans. After landing there, they returned to Missouri and a hero's welcome. Ragged but proud, they had covered more than 5,000 miles in their epic journey.

After winning two battles at Palo Alto and Resaca de la Palma, General Taylor was awaiting reinforcements and siege guns before advancing on Monterey.

Through intermediaries, Santa Anna, now in exile in Cuba, convinced President Polk that if he were passed through the American blockade, he would enter Mexico, seize power, and then negotiate the purchase of western lands and sign a peace treaty. Polk agreed, and in August 1846, Santa Anna arrived in Mexico.

True to his character, Santa Anna double-crossed Polk, denounced the Americans, seized power in Mexico City, and began raising new armies to drive the gringos out of Mexico.

Alexander W. Doniphan was a Missouri lawyer when war broke out. With no military experience he raised 1,000 men for the 1st Regiment of Missouri Mounted Volunteers. He led them on an epic march through northern Mexico. (Library of Congress)

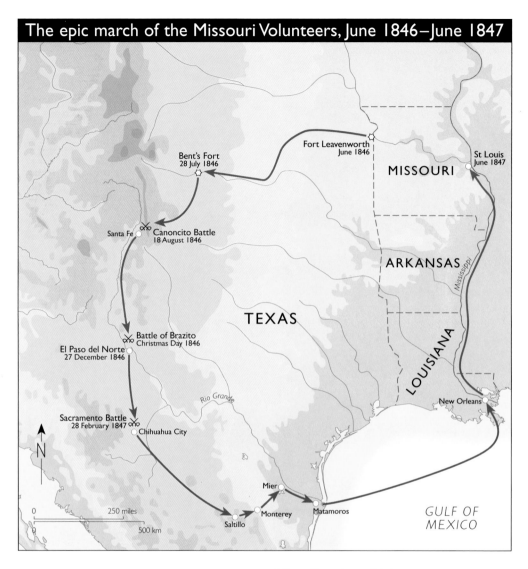

The epic march of the Missouri Volunteers, June 1846–June 1847

After marching west from Ft Leavenworth to Bent's Fort in Colorado, Colonel Alexander W. Doniphan turned south. After winning a skirmish at Canoncito, he occupied Santa Fe. Continuing south along the Rio Grande, he fought a sharp battle at Brazito, near the present-day city of El Paso, Texas. There he defeated a Mexican force of 1,200 men.

From the Pass of the North, Doniphan probed deeper into Chihuahua and on 28 February 1847, his Missourians defeated 3,000 Mexicans at Sacramento and he occupied the state capital, Chihuahua City. After another long, dusty march they linked up with Taylor's army at Monterey. From there it was on to Matamoros and a ship to New Orleans. Doniphan's contemporaries liked to compare his march to that of Xenophon, the Greek who led 10,000 troops to safety on a fighting 1,500-mile march through hostile Persian territory around 400 BC.

The Battle of Monterey

Taylor, now heavily reinforced with volunteer regiments, was stalled near the Rio Grande for lack of transport, and many of his new recruits had fallen ill with fever and dysentery. Under constant pressure from Polk to advance into Mexico, Taylor marched on Monterey with 6,000 of the more healthy regulars and volunteers, reaching the outskirts of the city on 19 September. More than 10,000 Mexican regulars under the command of General Ampudia had spent the intervening months fortifying the approaches to the city.

Taylor split his forces, sending General William Worth's Division to attack the fortified heights from the west and the south while his remaining troops attacked from the north-west. After fierce fighting and despite heavy losses, the Americans broke through the defenses and the Mexicans retreated into the city.

Some historians believe it was the Texans, who had had experience fighting in adobe and rock houses in Mexican cities, who taught the regulars the tactics of urban fighting. They would smash through a house wall with pickaxes, or blast holes through it with a 6-pounder cannonball. A timed explosive shell would then be fired through the opening, and when the shell exploded, infantry would rush in through the gap to

On 19 September, Taylor's army arrived before Monterey. The following day, General Worth's division moved south-west and cut the Saltillo Road, preventing Mexican reinforcements for General Ampudia's garrison of 10,000. Driving a Mexican force before him, on 21 September, Worth's men assaulted positions west of the city and captured fortified hills to the south. Butler's volunteers and Twigg's troops, attacking from the north-west, were first repulsed, but rallied and captured Fort Teneria.

On 22 September, after Worth's men had captured the heavily defended Bishop's Palace, Ampudia retreated into the city center. There followed two days of vicious house-to-house fighting until, on 24 September, the Mexican commander asked for surrender terms.

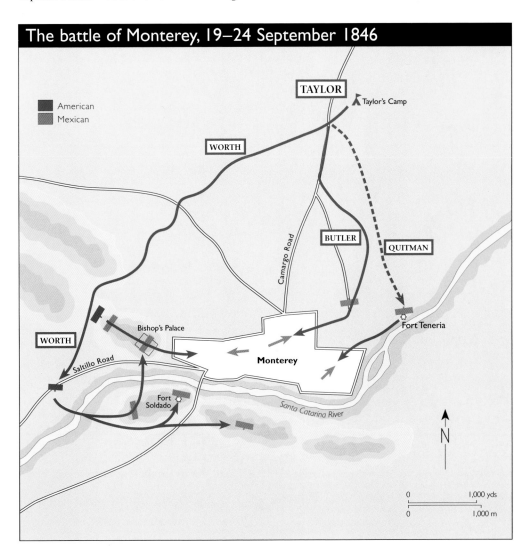

The battle of Monterey, 19–24 September 1846

American
Mexican

TAYLOR

Taylor's Camp

WORTH

Camargo Road

BUTLER

QUITMAN

Bishop's Palace

WORTH

Fort Teneria

Saltillo Road

Monterey

Fort Soldado

Santa Catarina River

N

0   1,000 yds
0   1,000 m

Fifty-one-year-old General Pedro de Ampudia was an experienced soldier who was appointed general in chief of the Mexican Army of the North. Although he fortified the city of Monterey, his defensive line was breached by a tenacious American attack. He surrendered, but he received terms 'too generous' from Taylor. (Archives Division, Texas State Library)

kill anyone still alive inside the building. Riflemen would then position themselves on the roof and snipe at the enemy in adjoining houses or streets. When one house had been cleared, the process was repeated on the next.

Fighting hand to hand and house to house, the Americans drove toward the center of the city. The end came when an American 10-inch mortar began dropping shells into the central plaza, causing Ampudia to ask for and receive a ceasefire.

On 25 September, Mexican troops abandoned Monterey and the Americans marched in. During the fighting, Taylor's men had suffered 120 killed and 333 wounded while the Mexicans reported more than 400 casualties.

At the end of 1846, most of northern Mexico had been secured by American forces. Polk, however, was outraged at the ceasefire signed by Taylor. The president believed it was too lenient and had enabled the Mexican army to escape. From that time on, he lost confidence in Taylor's ability to successfully prosecute the war.

The Battle of Buena Vista

In desperation, Polk turned to General Winfield Scott, a political enemy, for a solution to the Mexican dilemma. Scott, the most knowledgeable American soldier, proposed an amphibious operation which would land an American army in Vera Cruz, then strike west to capture Mexico City. Holding the Mexican capital by the throat, Scott believed, would force the Mexicans to sign a peace treaty. Polk, although fearing that Scott would become a national hero and a political rival, approved the plan.

General Scott was a man of gigantic ego and irascible temper who had many enemies in both military and political circles. Polk realized, however, that he was the one indispensable soldier who could win the war.

Since Scott would need the blooded regulars now serving with Taylor, the president ordered

that Taylor's forces be stripped to reinforce the new invasion plan. In January 1847, Taylor was reduced to guarding Monterey; General Worth's division of 4,000 regulars, two battalions of artillery, 1,000 cavalry, and many

Crusty and bold General Zachary Taylor was the opposite of Scott. A frontier soldier, his volunteer troops loved him and his informal ways, fondly calling him 'Old Rough and Ready.' In the front lines of the early battles, waving an old straw hat, he inspired his ill-trained volunteers with his courage and confidence. (Library of Congress)

Taylor launched a series of uncoordinated attacks that were bloodily repulsed and cost more than 20 percent of his army in casualties. His lack of technical skill was made up for by the tenacity of his men. After two days of fighting, the outer defenses of the city based on the Bishop's Palace were finally overcome and his battered troops entered the city. (Painting by Carl Nebel, Archives Division, Texas State Library)

volunteer infantry regiments were ordered to the coast to embark for Vera Cruz.

American generals were not immune to political rivalries, and Taylor, now a leading candidate for the Whig party nomination for the 1848 election, suspected a plot by Polk and Scott to destroy him politically. Although furious, Taylor refused to resign over what he considered an insult.

Two hundred fifty miles to the south, at San Luis Potosi, Santa Anna had gathered 20,000 ill-trained troops. Shortly after Taylor sent off the bulk of his veterans to Scott, Santa Anna's scouts acquired a bonanza. They captured a dispatch which not only outlined Scott's invasion plans but also listed the number of American troops remaining with Taylor. When the Mexican commander

LEFT Storming into the city, regulars and Texas volunteers fought house to house and street by street toward Monterey's Grand Plaza and finally forced their way to the center. One wearied soldier said: 'It was a hornet's nest, where every house was a fortress.' (Ann S.K. Brown University)

The battle of Buena Vista, 23 February 1847

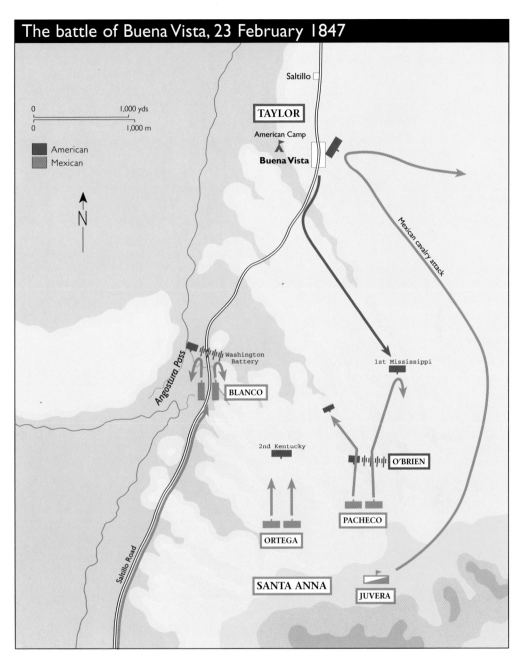

ABOVE On the morning of 23 February, General Santa Anna hurled 15,000 men against an outnumbered American army. At Angostura Pass on the Saltillo Road they were repulsed with heavy losses by fierce American artillery fire, but the Mexican right wing successfully tore into the American center and left flank, overrunning an artillery battery and panicking a volunteer regiment. While Taylor's left disintegrated, his center made a fighting withdrawal. Mexican cavalry swept east of the mountains and attacked supply wagons at Hacienda Buena Vista, but they met determined resistance and were driven back. The American center stabilized and after the 3rd US Artillery regiment broke a final attack on the left front, the tide of battle turned. By mid-afternoon a second Mexican attack was broken and Santa Anna ordered a retreat.

The three-gun artillery battery commanded by Captain John Paul Jones O'Brien with the 2nd Indiana Volunteers on his right flank was attacked by 7,000 Mexican lancers and infantry. The Indianans broke but the artillerymen fought until most were killed or wounded and the guns were taken. (Sam Chamberlain, San Jacinto Museum of History Association)

learned of Taylor's depleted force, he decided to attack and destroy the weakened Americans. Then, he believed, flushed with victory, he would be able to rally the Mexican people and turn south to crush Scott at Vera Cruz.

On 2 February 1847, Santa Anna headed his army north. The march was mostly across desert country, where water and grazing land was scarce. Rations and forage were in short supply and his men, inadequately clothed, suffered terribly from the cold. On 21 February, his tired troops reached La Encarnacion, only a day's march from Taylor's defensive position. More than 5,000 had fallen by the wayside, either through illness, fatigue, or desertion. Worse, the element of surprise had been lost after Texas Ranger Captain Ben McCulloch slipped past Mexican sentries and climbed a hill overlooking the Mexican camp. From there, he made an accurate count of the enemy

force and galloped back to Taylor with the information. With this intelligence, Taylor deployed his remaining 4,700 troops in defensive positions at Angostura Pass near the hacienda Buena Vista, seven miles south of Saltillo. Then he waited for the attack.

On 22 February, the 15,000-strong Mexican army deployed along the Saltillo Road. That afternoon they attacked the American left flank nestled in rugged hills and were repulsed by accurate infantry fire. The fighting slackened as darkness fell, and throughout the night the troops were pelted with cold rain.

At daybreak, Santa Anna launched his main attacks. Attempting to break through Angostura Pass, the Mexicans were decimated by artillery under the command of Major John Washington. Another attack on the American left flank met with initial success but was soon shattered by infantry reinforcements and the always devastating fire of the light artillery guns, whose grapeshot blew gaping holes in attacking infantry and cavalry.

Santa Anna, suffering more than 3,500 casualties and needing to keep his army intact to fight Scott, gave up northern

Buena Vista was the decisive battle in the northern
Mexico campaign. The raw American volunteers showed
they could maintain discipline under pressure. The
artillerymen, commanded by West Point graduates,
demonstrated that they could shoot and maneuver
quickly and accurately. The battle was a personal defeat
for Santa Anna , since 'Taylor's luck held.' (Painting by
Carl Nebel, Archives Division, Texas State Library)

Mexico and retreated to Mexico City. Taylor,
an inept tactician, lost 650 men but won a
decisive victory because of the steadfastness
of his infantry and the expertise of his
gunners. For all practical purposes, the war
in the north had ended.

The San Patricios

There were two anomalies among the
military units who fought in the northern
battles and later in Scott's campaign. They
were the San Patricios and the Texas Rangers.

The regular US army coupled a harsh
discipline with a sometimes vicious
discrimination against Irish immigrant
soldiers. Their religion, language, and
demeanor were often ridiculed by Protestant
officers and non commissioned officers alike,
and they were often brutally punished for
what they considered minor offenses.

While the American army was camped along the Rio Grande across from Matamoros, more than a few Irishmen believed they were lashed or bucked and gagged unjustly. An Irish sergeant named John Riley, tall, blue-eyed, and with a mop of curly black hair and a gift of the gab, finally had enough of the ill treatment. A former artilleryman in the British army, one night he swam across the river and was welcomed by his fellow Catholics in the Mexican army. Brandishing free whiskey, promising the favors of nubile senoritas, and offering 320 acres of good farming land,

Riley enticed more than 200 Irishmen and a few German immigrants to desert and join the army of their fellow Catholics.

The deserters were trained as artillerymen and named the Batallon de San Patricio after the patron saint of Ireland. They flew a banner of green silk decorated with a golden harp and the words 'Erin go Bragh' (Ireland forever) on one side and a picture of Saint Patrick and the words San Patricio on the other. Riley was commissioned a lieutenant in the Mexican army, and as the San Patricios gained fame for valor in combat, he was eventually promoted to colonel.

The battalion first fought against their former comrades during the battle for Monterey. In ensuing battles at Buena Vista, Cerro Gordo, and Churubusco they gained a reputation as the most deadly and courageous gunners in the Mexican army. Theirs was a daring born of desperation, because they fought 'with a rope around their necks.'

At Angostura Pass at Buena Vista, one third of the battalion were casualties. During their final fight at Churubusco, they suffered 60 percent casualties after heroically trying to repulse American attacks. Seventy men, including Riley, were captured.

Following court-martial, 20 of them, including Riley, were each given 50 lashes on their bare backs and had a D branded on their cheek with a hot iron. Then they were released. Twenty more were almost immediately hanged. On 13 September 1847, the remaining 30 were positioned on wagons facing Chapultepec Castle. A rope with a hangman's knot was fastened around their necks. When the Stars and Stripes were hoisted over the castle battlements, the mules pulling the wagons were swatted and leaped forward, and the San Patricios dropped to their deaths as traitors and deserters.

To this day, the San Patricios are honored in Mexico as national heroes. There is a monument in Mexico City where twice a year, on Saint Patrick's day and the anniversary of the battle of Churubusco, bands and officials of both Mexico and the

Republic of Ireland pay homage to the fallen soldiers of the Batallon de San Patricio.

The Texas Rangers

For the previous 15 years Texas Rangers had been fighting Mexican soldiers. Many were related to those who had been butchered at the Alamo or Goliad and to them the war was an opportunity for revenge. Their quality of mercy was never strained, for they had none.

The Rangers had their origin as a paramilitary force organized in 1820 to patrol land around Texas settlements and to pursue and destroy Indian raiders and predatory bandits. In these affrays, no quarter was given or received. All volunteers, they fought with military discipline but wore no uniforms and paid no homage to military 'fuss and feathers.'

Led by experienced fighters, well armed, dressed in frontier garb, excellent riders and lethal marksmen, the Texas Rangers provided their own horses and weapons. They proved invaluable to both Taylor and Scott for reconnaissance, as shock troops, and, most importantly, as anti-guerrilla fighters.

In the brutal guerrilla war along American supply lines, unfortunately their excesses detracted from their stellar military performance. Taylor, who had needed them badly, complained: 'There is scarcely a crime that has not been reported to me as committed by them.' They were reviled by Mexicans as *Los diablos Tejanos* (Texas devils). Before Monterey, in the dark during a rainstorm, they climbed up the steep face of fortified Independence Hill and cut the Mexican defenders to pieces with Bowie knives and pistols.

Fighting guerrillas or bandits (the two were indistinguishable) who plagued Scott's supply line from Vera Cruz, the Rangers adopted Comanche tactics. Locating a guerrilla force, they would swoop down on an enemy camp at dawn. Riding at the gallop with their Colt revolvers blazing, they would overrun and kill everyone in the

camp. With superior weapons, led by charismatic frontier chieftains, and believing they were the best fighting men on earth, they created a legend that lives to this day.

Vera Cruz

On 9 March 1847, a fleet of 100 ships transported Major General Winfield Scott and 12,000 men to Mexican shores a few miles south of Vera Cruz, Mexico's major seaport and the gateway to its capital. As bands played, the troops were rowed ashore in specially built landing craft, out of range of the cannon of the formidable San Juan de Ulua fort that guarded the harbor.

Scott was in a hurry to take Vera Cruz before the dreaded yellow fever season began in April.

His troops encircled the city and cut off its water supply. Then he had some of the fleet's big guns transported ashore. Captain Robert E. Lee, an engineer officer, after a reconnaissance, placed land batteries around the city perimeter.

From 22 March, army artillery, the naval guns on land, and the guns of the fleet in the harbor, bombarded the port for five days, reducing much of the city to rubble and causing the Mexican commandant to surrender. Scott had his harbor and his logistical base secured.

While the American general prepared to follow the route of Cortez and his Conquistadors, Santa Anna was raising a new army to oppose him. Within a month of his drubbing at Buena Vista, the self-styled 'Napoleon of the West' had suppressed opposition in Mexico City, reorganized the

Seated backward on wagons, the San Patricios, with ropes around their necks, heard a triumphant shout by the Americans. The stars and stripes now flew over the heights of Chapultepec. Then the mules were given a whack, leaped forward and the San Patricios died. (Sam Chamberlain, San Jacinto Museum of History Association)

army command and promised his people he would drive the Americans into the sea.

By the first week in April, Santa Anna had deployed his new army around the mountain pass of Cerro Gordo, through which the highway to Mexico City passed. With a river and high bluffs to the right of the highway and steep hills to the left, Santa Anna placed guns and infantry on the high ground each side of the road. He believed the Americans would have to advance along the highway and could be cut to pieces from crossfire.

Lee and other reconnaissance teams, however, had found a path around the fortified hills on Santa Anna's left flank. On 17 April, Scott mounted a fake attack on the Mexican right while his main force, undetected, followed the path until they were in the left rear of the Mexican defenses. Under the unexpected attack the Mexican troops began a frenzied retreat.

The Americans inflicted hundreds of casualties, captured 3,000 prisoners, and confiscated large stores of ammunition and provisions while themselves losing less than 500 men. Scott, however, was suddenly faced with a serious loss of manpower. In May, seven state regiments of 12-month volunteers, veterans of Monterey, Vera Cruz and Cerro Gordo, announced that their time was expiring and demanded to be shipped home. Scott's pleas notwithstanding, they were adamant, and the general was reluctantly forced to let them leave. The American commander, deep in Mexican territory, now had an army of something less than 7,000 men.

Despite his thinned ranks, Scott marched his army to Puebla, the second largest city in Mexico, and took it, to little opposition, on 15 May. With 2,000 of his men now ill and with a supply line threatened by guerrilla forces, Scott could barely field 5,000. Fearing an attack by Santa Anna's growing army, he waited in Puebla for reinforcements. Soon he was joined by diplomat Nicolas P. Trist, sent by Polk to negotiate a peace treaty when, if ever, the Mexicans surrendered.

In July, other, more welcome American reinforcements began to arrive and by 7 August, the American army had been built up to almost 14,000 men (although more than 3,000 were convalescing or too sick to march). Like Cortez three centuries before, Scott was undeterred from attacking a hostile capital with inferior numbers. Mexico City boasted a population of almost a quarter of a million people and the city was garrisoned by an army three times the size of Scott's forces.

Leaving his sick behind in Puebla, and the odds notwithstanding, Scott gave the order to advance. The army hiked 75 miles up the road toward the capital, winding around mountain passes until they had ascended to an altitude of 10,000 feet. Stopping to catch their breath, the soldiers could view the snow-covered summit of Popocatepetl volcano stretching 18,000 feet into the sky.

Three thousand feet below lay the green and beautiful Valley of Mexico. Shimmering in the sun were the large lakes of Texcoco, Chalco, and Xochimilco. Through the mountain haze they could see the spires of the great cathedral and the palaces of the Dons. It was, they thought, magnificent, but looming with danger were the high walls of the Molino

del Rey and the cliffs of Chapultepec Palace. It was there, they knew, that the future of both the United States and Mexico would be decided.

Contreras and Churubusco

If Santa Anna was not a talented soldier, he was a persistent one. Back in Mexico City he again squelched opposition and began raising yet another army that was to total between 25,000 and 30,000 men. He also began fortifying the approaches to the city.

The Mexican capital would be a tough nut to crack for Scott's troops. It was surrounded by marshlands, the remainders of ancient

The landward side of Vera Cruz was heavily fortified. Stout stone walls surrounded the city, and before them trenches were filled with sharp wooden stakes to impale attackers. Nine forts, supported by scores of heavy artillery batteries, promised to meet assault troops with a rain of shells. Scott borrowed heavy guns from the warships, set up land batteries, and in coordination with the Navy launched a furious cannonade upon the city, forcing its surrender. (Painting by Carl Nebel, Archives Division, Texas State Library)

The first major amphibious landing in US military history was accomplished on 9 March 1847, when troops were rowed ashore unopposed to beaches south of Vera Cruz. Just three years short of a century later, Americans and their British allies powered ashore in Normandy. Both campaigns led to final victory after hard fighting. (Library of Congress)

lakes. To approach the city it was necessary to traverse the many causeways, which could easily be interdicted by artillery. The Mexicans erected strong redoubts to the north and south, but the main fortifications were placed at El Penon, a hill where artillery could command the main road from Vera Cruz. Along this road, Santa Anna believed, the Americans would attack.

As Scott's army of 10,000 approached the city, the general faced a dilemma. To continue along the highway, he would be forced to make a frontal attack on El Penon. To shift his forces to the north would require a 40-mile march around Lake Texcoco only to confront strong defenses at Guadalupe Hidalgo, which was garrisoned by 5,000 troops and heavy guns. To move south by way of Mexicalcingo would leave his right flank and rear open to attacks from troops disgorging from El Penon.

Scott sent Robert E. Lee, whose military reputation was soaring, to make a long and daring personal reconnaissance below the southern defenses of the city. After dodging Mexican patrols and reconnoitering the tangled terrain, Lee found a way around the strongest Mexican defenses.

He reported that the army could abandon the main highway and follow a rough trail that wound to the south of Lake Chalco and Lake Xochimilco and bypassed the outer defenses. Scott agreed with Lee's plan and on 14 August, his infantry and cavalry marched surefootedly along the trail while the artillery and supply wagons bumped along, rattling but intact.

On 17 August, the advance guard under General Worth captured the key town of San Augustin, nestled below the rugged ancient lava flow called the Pedregal. Alarmed, Santa Anna shifted his forces to meet the unexpected threat. He stripped the fortress at El Penon, moved troops and guns south of the city and set up new defensive positions along the road east of the lava beds.

As Worth was entering San Augustin, Santa Anna was ordering General Gabriel Valencia to take up positions near the town of Contreras, on the west side of the lava beds. Santa Anna changed his mind the following day and ordered Valencia to retreat. The general, however, disobeyed the order and decided to stand at Contreras. The following day, 19 August, Scott split up his troops and ordered Worth to feint an attack on the left of the Pedregal. Meanwhile, American engineers cut a road across the lava field to the west, enabling the bulk of their forces to launch an attack on Contreras which again outflanked their main defenses.

As they moved into position, the separated American forces left a wide gap between them, exposing their flanks to counterattack. If Santa Anna had had the boldness to exploit this gap and attacked, he might have defeated the Americans in detail, but the 'Napoleon of the West' lost his nerve. He retreated toward Churubusco, which anchored the north-eastern part of his

defenses. Again he ordered Valencia to retreat, but the stubborn general refused his orders once more.

During a rain-filled night, Scott's scouts located a ravine that wound around to the rear of Valencia's position. The following morning, the Americans faked a frontal attack while the main body followed the ravine and came up in the rear of the Mexican troops. They launched an immediate attack and in a brisk fight lasting less than half an hour, Scott's men inflicted more than 1,000 casualties on the Mexican defenders. They took 800 prisoners, overran 20 artillery pieces, and captured a herd of mules. American losses were less than 100.

Santa Anna, retreating to Churubusco, ordered Valencia shot. He then commanded that the main bridge over the Churubusco River and the fortified San Mateo convent be held at all costs. In both places the defiant San Patricios manned key artillery positions.

After taking Contreras, Scott quickly decided to pursue the fleeing Mexicans and unite his forces before Churubusco. In their second battle of the day, the tired Americans suffered heavily from infantry and artillery fire during their assault on both the bridge and the convent. They launched charge after charge until they penetrated part of Churubusco's defenses, after which Mexican soldiers attempted to raise a white flag and surrender. With curses, the enraged San Patricios tore it down and continued to fight under their emerald banner, until American bayonets ripped it down and the position finally fell.

On 20 August, the Mexican army had a grim day. They had already lost two battles and more than a third of their troops, either from enemy fire, surrender, or desertion. More than 4,000 were dead or wounded and 3,000 had been taken prisoner. Eight of the prisoners were generals, two of whom had once been presidents of Mexico, and as the

Robert E. Lee, shown here in 1865 while commanding the Confederate Army, as a young engineer officer made daring reconnaissance trips behind the Mexican lines, enabling Scott to skirt the strongest enemy positions. (Library of Congress)

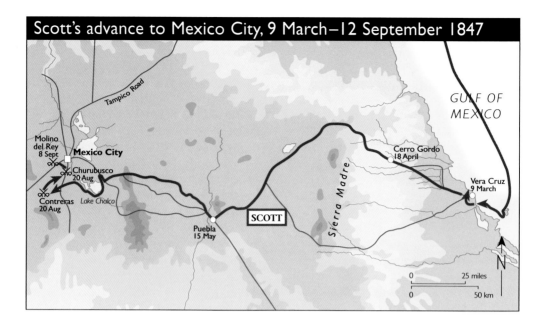

Scott's advance to Mexico City, 9 March–12 September 1847

Cerro Gordo or 'Fat Hill' was strategically located on the main road leading to Mexico City. Santa Anna was confident he could stop the Americans there since his guns could rain havoc on any troops hiking along the road. However, the Americans found a path around the Mexican left flank and rear, and routed the defenders. Fleeing the battle Santa Anna abandoned his wooden left leg. (Painting by Carl Nebel, Archives Division, Texas State Library)

day ended, the Americans were camped less than four miles from Mexico City.

Scott's men, however, were exhausted from forced marches, constant fighting, and debilitating illnesses. Since marching from Vera Cruz, the Americans had lost more than 1,000 effectives. While his men rested, Scott

Following the Americans' first major amphibious landing below Vera Cruz, Scott laid siege to the port, which surrendered on 27 March. Leading an army never numbering more than 10,000 effectives, Scott made a fighting advance toward Mexico's capital, winning a major battle at Cerro Gordo on 18 April. He occupied Puebla on 15 May and awaited reinforcements. In early August, bedevilled by guerrillas attempting to cut his tenuous supply lines, he marched on. Reaching the outskirts of Mexico City, he awaited reconnaissance reports from Robert E. Lee.

When Lee advised an attack from the south, the army skirted below Lake Chalco and Xochimilco and then struck north. They defeated Mexican defenders at Contreras and Churbusco on 20 August and at Molino del Rey on 8 September. The Americans were then poised for the war's climactic battle.

sent a message to Santa Anna, demanding he surrender Mexico City. The Mexican leader, stalling for time, hinted at a peace settlement and warned that an attack on the capital would scatter the government and make peace negotiations impossible. Taking the hint, Scott offered a ceasefire during which time a peaceful settlement could be negotiated.

On 24 August, both sides signed an armistice. Its provisions included an exchange of prisoners which overwhelmingly worked to the benefit of

Santa Anna's depleted army. Both sides agreed that during negotiations neither side would reinforce their armies. Scott complied; Santa Anna did not. Instead he frantically attempted to raise more troops and bolster the inner defenses of the capital.

The truce also allowed the Americans to purchase food supplies from the large markets in Mexico City. This provision too was not honored. When an unarmed American provision train entered the city to purchase food, it was driven off by enraged Mexican soldiers and citizens. Santa Anna apologized, but took no action to prevent further attacks.

Scott ignored the violations in order to continue negotiations between American peace commissioners and Mexican government officials. After two weeks of

American troops cut a road through a lava field, the Pedregal, up to Contreras Hill, where the Mexicans were entrenched. American forces became separated during the advance and were in danger of being defeated in detail. The following day, however, Santa Anna lost his nerve and retreated. Against orders, General Gabriel Valencia made a stand but the Americans soon routed his forces at bayonet point. (Carl Nebel, Archives Division, Texas State Library)

dithering with the Mexican delegates, who rejected every American proposal, Scott realized he had been tricked and he terminated the armistice. Santa Anna countered with a ringing speech of defiance.

Scott determined to attack the city and moved his rested troops toward the south-west causeways which led to the center of the capital. Blocking his way were fortifications around the Molino del Rey (King's Mill), an industrial complex which was said to be producing weapons for the Mexican army. The Molino consisted of more than 200 yards of stone buildings. A report, later proved to be false, stated that all the church bells of Mexico City were being melted down in the Molino and recast as cannon.

Two heavily fortified positions anchored the Mexican defensive line. On the left flank was an old abandoned flour mill, the Molino, and on the right, the walls of the Casa Mata. Between the positions, Santa Anna had massed most of his artillery.

General Worth's division of 3,000 men was ordered to storm both positions and open the road to the capital. Worth created a party of 500 volunteers selected from each

infantry regiment in the army. On the morning of 8 September, American artillery shelled the Molino while the storming party, under heavy fire from Mexican infantry and artillery, attacked.

At first, although taking numerous casualties, the Americans broke into the Mexican line and captured an artillery battery. However, with their ranks reduced by casualties, they were forced to retreat when the defenders counterattacked. The storming party, under Major George Wright, was raked by continuing enemy fire and the major and 10 of the other 14 officers were struck down. More than half of the elite 500 littered the ground in front of the Molino.

Worth then ordered his main force to assault all along the Mexican line. The Americans fired a volley, then, screaming war cries and curses, smashed their way into the

Santa Anna had his men fortify a convent near a bridge crossing the Churubusco River. The American advance was stopped temporarily by the frenzied soldiers of the San Patricio Battalion. They were men fighting 'with a noose around their necks.' Finally, the Mexicans broke and Scott won his second battle of the day. (Painting by Carl Nebel, Archives Division, Texas State Library)

defenses. Rifles and pistols blasted at close range quickly gave way to musket butts and slashing bayonets as bloody hand-to-hand fighting raged through the rooms and hallways of the old mill.

At the other end of the line, at the Casa Mata, the first American attack was repulsed with heavy losses. The flying batteries were rushed to the front, where they opened a furious barrage on the Mexican positions with explosive shells and canister as the Americans attacked again. Although the Mexicans fought with stubborn valor and most of the defenders died at their posts, with repeated American attacks the Casa Mata was finally overrun and captured.

By mid-morning, after two hours of fighting, Worth's men had occupied the entire Mexican defense line. Worth had lost 116 dead and 671 wounded, more than a third of the soldiers who had made the attacks. The Mexicans had fought with great bravery but had suffered more than 2,000 killed and wounded, 700 captured, and

Mexican troops fighting behind parapets at the Tete de Pont bridgehead over the Churubusco River sent a hailstorm of bullets into the American ranks, causing heavy casualties. The Americans, however, continued to advance over the bodies of their dead until the exhausted defenders retreated into Mexico City. (Library of Congress)

an estimated 2,000 deserters. Many of those who fled the Molino probably rejoined the Mexican garrison holding out at the inner defenses of Mexico City.

Neither Worth nor Santa Anna gained any glory from the battle. As they mourned the heavy butcher's bill, many American officers were irate at Worth's handling of the battle. His attacks, they said, were clumsy and uncoordinated. Santa Anna, on the other hand, had retired the night before to the National Palace in Mexico City in order, he claimed, to 'get a good night's sleep.' Others accused him of yet another dalliance. They recalled that similar events at San Jacinto in 1836 and at Vera Cruz during the French invasion of 1837 had caught him

A fortified foundry, Molino del Rey, or King's Mill, was part of the western defenses around Chapultepec Castle, the key to the defenses of Mexico City. As a forlorn hope of 500 picked men charged the Mexican lines, inside the foundry, workers were still casting Mexican cannon. Suffering heavily, the Americans took the walls at bayonet point. The road to Chapultepec was now open. (Painting by Carl Nebel, Archives Division, Texas State Library)

flagrante delicto. His amours, they charged, had contributed to both military disasters. In any event, the generalissimo arrived within a mile of the Molino just in time to join the retreat of the survivors of his defeated forces.

The following day, 9 September, General Scott summoned Robert E. Lee to accompany him on a reconnaissance of the inner ring of defenses of Mexico City. Accompanied by staff officers and engineers, they first observed the Nino Perdido Road and the San Antonio Causeway to the south-east of the city. Scott spent two more days observing the Mexican defenses to the west, of which the

Lee believed. All but one of the senior generals and engineers agreed with him.

Then, the young Lieutenant Pierre G.T. Beauregard, who would later become a general in the Confederate Army, spoke up. Passionately, the Louisiana Creole argued that Santa Anna expected an attack from the south and that he had many of his big guns positioned to dominate the southern causeways. Fake an attack from the south, he argued, then strike at Chapultepec. Brigadier General Franklin Pierce of the New Hampshire Volunteers, who would later defeat Winfield Scott for the presidency of the United States, agreed. Scott had already made up his mind. 'Gentlemen,' he said, 'we will attack from the west. We will take Chapultepec Castle.'

grim, looming Chapultepec Castle was the key.

On the evening of 11 September, Scott called a council of war with his most senior and trusted officers. The general informed them that he preferred to attack the castle, but he asked: 'What are your opinions?' Robert E. Lee spoke first. Contradicting his superior officer, Lee proposed an attack from the south, driving up the San Antonio Causeway to the heart of the city. Attacking the castle on its high ground would be too costly in casualties,

U.S. Grant: From the depths to the heights

General William Tecumseh Sherman said it best: 'Grant's whole character was a mystery even to himself; a combination of strength and weakness not paralleled by any whom I have read in ancient or modern history.'

Ulysses Simpson Grant was born on an Ohio farm in 1822 and spent his early years helping his father bring in crops. As a youth he showed no interest in the military, but when his father secured for him an appointment to West Point Military Academy, he grudgingly agreed to enter the school.

He disliked the academy, with its spit and polish and difficult curriculum. He did, however, shine in mathematics, but was a diffident scholar in other studies. On horseback he became transfigured: a shy, smallish man on the ground, he was a commanding equestrian in the saddle. The man who would later command all the armies of the United States did not like the army.

After graduating in the middle of his class in 1843, Grant informed his classmates that he planed to resign his commission at an early date and find a job as a mathematics teacher. The delicate, fair-skinned, five-foot eight-inch-tall lieutenant, who was once described as looking 'like a doll,' was not rated highly enough to be assigned to the coveted engineers or field artillery branches. He was instead assigned to the 4th Infantry to quartermaster and commissary duties.

When war broke out between the United States and Mexico, Grant determined to do his duty in spite of his opposition to the conflict. He later wrote: 'I regard the war as one of the most unjust ever waged by a stronger against a weaker nation.' Grant considered the war 'a conspiracy to acquire territory out of which slave states might be formed for the American Union.'

In September 1845, the 4th Infantry joined Zachary Taylor's army near Corpus Christi, Texas. Camping there to pass the time before marching to the Rio Grande, the officers formed a theatrical troupe. In a production of *Othello*, Grant played the gentle lady Desdemona. Pictured in well-known photos taken during the Civil War, it is difficult to imagine the rumpled, bearded, grim-faced general who, one observer remarked, 'looked like he was about to ram his head through a brick wall,' playing the part of the delicate wife of a Moorish general.

When the fighting started, Grant wrote that he was determined to do his duty as a soldier to bring victory to his country. Before Fort Texas on the Rio Grande on 2 May

Although Lieutenant Sam (Ulysses S.) Grant, a West Pointer, thought the war was unjustified, he fought bravely through all the major battles. (Library of Congress)

1846, he first heard the sound of hostile cannon, and later recalled: 'I felt sorry that I had enlisted.'

His baptism of fire came on 8 May during the battle of Palo Alto, when a cannon ball decapitated a soldier standing near him. The following day, Grant was given command of his company as they marched to the relief of Fort Texas.

During the ensuing battle of Resaca de la Palma, he led his company in a successful charge, backed up by the Flying Artillery. In August, when Taylor began his march to Monterey, Grant, much to his disgust, was placed in charge of the regimental mule train. Frustrated, Grant wrote that he had never used a profane expletive in his life but 'I would have the charity to excuse those who may have done so, if they were in charge of a train of Mexican pack mules.'

After his regimental adjutant was killed during a charge before Monterey, Grant took over those duties and by 23 September, he had undergone a metamorphosis about combat and was gratified to battle his way into the city alongside his regiment.

During house-to-house fighting, the 4th ran low on ammunition and Grant volunteered to ride through a gauntlet of gunfire to bring up additional supplies. Through a hellfire of shot and shell, hooking a foot over his saddle with one arm around his horse's neck, he clung to the side of his mount Comanche style and galloped back to the supply wagons. He soon returned to the fight with a wagon-load of ammunition.

In March 1847, Grant, who had been transferred to Scott's army, splashed ashore with the first troops to land on the beach south of Vera Cruz. To his dismay, his efficiency as a mule train driver resulted in his being made permanent quartermaster for his regiment. During the battles of Cerro Gordo, Contreras, and Churubusco, Grant was relegated to guarding the mules and the supply wagons.

When the American army advanced toward Mexico City, he volunteered to help reconnoiter the city's defenses. In his memoirs written some 40 years later, Grant praised the reconnaissance reports of his future nemesis, Robert E. Lee as 'perfect.' Lee, in his report, noticed the work of 'Lieutenant Grant … who was usefully employed.' Ironically, when the Civil War erupted 15 years later, Lee refused the command of the Union armies which Grant would lead to victory against him after four years of bitter fighting.

. In the attack on Molino del Rey, Grant left his mules and joined in the assault. During the hand-to-hand fighting, he encountered the brother of Julia Dent, his fiancée. Lieutenant Fred Dent, laying with a bullet in his thigh, said he could await the surgeons, so Grant hurried back into the thick of the fighting. By nightfall, the battle had been won, but at a terrible cost in casualties. For his gallantry during the attack, Grant was brevetted a first lieutenant.

He missed the fighting during the assault on Chapultepec, but when that position was taken, he was one of the first to arrive before the gate of the San Cosme Causeway, which led to the center of Mexico City. The San Cosme was the same elevated road that Cortez had used during his retreat from the Aztec capital 300 years previously. The defenders had placed guns and infantry to sweep the approaches along the road. Grant realized that the enemy position had to be destroyed if the American attack was to succeed.

He later wrote: 'I found a church … that looked to me as if the belfry would command the ground back of … San Cosme.' The young lieutenant commandeered a mountain howitzer and a number of men from the Voltiguers Regiment. He ordered the gun disassembled and parceled out the components to his men. To dodge the road, which was swept by enemy fire, Grant and his men slipped to the south and carried the howitzer parts through several ditches, wading through waist-deep water. Coming up behind the church, Grant politely knocked on the door. When a priest opened the door and peeked out at the muddy, sweat-soaked lieutenant, he at first refused admittance.

In his memoirs, Grant was perhaps too polite to write about his persuasive measures, merely stating that the priest 'began to see his duty in the same light that I did and opened the door.'

The Americans manhandled the howitzer parts up the winding, narrow stairway to the belfry and reassembled the gun. Grant later wrote: 'We were not more than two or three hundred yards from San Cosme.' Opening fire, the Americans dropped shell after explosive shell onto the heads of the San Cosme defenders.

In the meantime, the American troops who had been tunneling through adobe houses on the north side of the causeway reached the San Cosme gate. After Grant's bombardment had silenced the Mexican guns and raked and spread panic among the infantry defenders, the Americans were able to carry the position by assault. At the same time, other troops captured the Belen Gate and by the evening of 13 September, Scott's army had advanced to the heart of Mexico City. The following day, the capital capitulated as the remaining Mexican troops retreated from the city. As a result of his action, Grant was brevetted captain. For all practical purposes, the fighting was over.

When the war ended, Grant returned home and on 22 August 1848, he married his long-time sweetheart, Julia Dent. A few years later, while stationed in California and separated from his wife, out of loneliness and boredom, he took to the bottle. In 1854, under a cloud caused by his excessive drinking, he resigned his commission.

Grant rejoined Julia and with his family settled in St. Louis, Missouri, for the next six years. During that time, he failed miserably both as a businessman and as a farmer. In 1860, he and his family moved to Galena, Illinois, where he worked as a clerk in his father's small leather store. In 1860, Grant was a broken, middle-aged man, cursed with failure and disappointment. Behind his back, neighbors referred to him not as Ulysses, but rather as 'Useless Grant.'

When the Civil War broke out in 1861 and the Union was desperate for experienced officers, Grant was commissioned a colonel of Illinois volunteers and was quickly raised to brigadier general. He had early successes, particularly in forcing the surrender of Fort Donelson, an important Confederate fort on the Cumberland River in Tennessee. He was promoted to major general, but in April 1862, his fortunes plummeted and he was nearly shelved when he barely escaped defeat during the bloody battle at Shiloh, Tennessee.

President Lincoln, suffering incompetent and reluctant generals, supported Grant. When told of Grant's drinking, Lincoln asked for the name of his brand of whiskey so he could send a keg to all of his generals. 'That man fights,' said Lincoln.

In July 1863, Grant captured the fortress of Vicksburg, the key to control of the Mississippi River. Shortly afterwards, he was given command of all the more than one million Union troops. Attacking Robert E. Lee in Virginia, Grant suffered appalling casualties: more than 6,000 Union soldiers fell in less than one hour at Cold Harbor. Grant weathered the cries of 'Butcher' and gradually wore down the thinning Confederate forces. Hailed as the hero who won the war, Grant was elected President in 1868 and was re-elected in 1872. After retirement, he made bad investments and became bankrupt and deeply in debt. Although suffering horribly from throat cancer, he wrote his memoirs to pay his debts. Four days after he finished them, he died, in July 1885.

Progress and stagnation

The Mexicans

The greatest obstacle for the Mexican government in forging a united front against the American invaders was the prevailing concept of *patria chica*, which translates as 'small homeland.' Divided by race, caste, language, and geography, Mexicans gave their loyalty to their family, close friends, village, linguistic group, or region. The concept of Mexican-ness or loyalty to the government in Mexico City was foreign to most. Spread over vast areas and separated by mountains, jungle, and desert, many Mexicans were both ignorant of and indifferent to the problems of their central government. Many Mexicans also regarded

While some Mexicans fought bitterly against the Americans, others collaborated both economically and socially. A peaceful fandango where American soldiers danced with senoritas was not uncommon. (Sam Chamberlain, San Jacinto Museum of History Association)

Santa Anna with a special hatred, and revolts against his government were endemic in many regions.

Patria chica was also reflected in the high rate of desertion among Mexican soldiers. Hungry, ill, only partially trained or equipped, and held in contempt by their officers, conscripts had little reason to fight the fierce Americanos. At the first opportunity, many slipped away from camp to find their way back to their home village.

While many Mexicans fought bravely against the invaders, there were others who actively collaborated with the Americans. Hundreds of Mexican men and women were hired by the American army to provide information about Mexican fortifications and troop movements. For example, Scott's intelligence officers hired a troop of 200 renegades and political dissenters to fight the guerrillas plaguing his supply line from Vera Cruz.

Others readily sold food, forage, horses, and mules to American quartermasters. Some hired themselves out as guides through a country unknown to the invaders. For a fee, numbers of Mexican women functioned as washerwomen, cooks, nurses, and sexual partners for American servicemen. Their services were indistinguishable from those of the soldaderas who succored Mexican soldiers.

Collaboration also reached into the highest ranks of state governments. In the north, the governors in Chihuahua, Coahuila, and Tamaulipas continued economic ties with the Americans. In the south, Chiapas and Tabasco refused to aid the central government, while the Yucatán rose in revolt. From 1847 to the end of hostilities, a peasant revolt in central Mexico further sapped that country's resistance to the invader.

When Napoleon said that an army marched on its stomach, he might have added that it marched only as far as its finances would take it. While internal dissent kept politicians playing musical chairs in Mexico City, the war effort was starving for funds. With the opening of hostilities in 1846, the Catholic Church pledged one million pesos to support the war effort of the already bankrupt government. It was little enough for a war that would ultimately cost 100 million pesos.

The American naval blockade not only prevented Mexico from purchasing needed weapons, it also cut off all sources of revenue from exports and customs duties, reducing public revenues by 50 percent. In desperation the Mexican government stopped payment of government salaries, pensions, and debt obligations. In an effort to raise funds they requested loans from states and cities, but *patria chica* remained an obstacle, and little help came from the outlands.

The Mexican government then seized Church property to use as collateral in an attempt to raise a badly needed 15 million pesos. This action caused a rebellion by Church adherents called Polkos, most of whom were militia officers from Mexico City. Santa Anna, diverted from attempting

to rebuild an army to fight Scott, quelled the rebellion by repudiating the seizure of Church property. Later he forced the Church to contribute two million pesos to his government. When new taxes could not be collected from an impoverished economy, Santa Anna simply seized needed supplies, giving worthless markers as payment.

Many Mexicans began to urge peace; they were willing to give up half their country in exchange for American dollars, which they hoped would mend their broken economy.

Financial disaster, combined with the disruption of domestic and international trade, the destruction of major cities and industries during the fighting, and the seizures of foodstuffs and other goods by both armies led to chronic hunger among much of the population.

Agriculture was the linchpin of Mexico's economy. Most of the production came from large estates worked by peons who were kept in constant debt by the haciendados. Unless a hacienda was located in the war zone, however, life went on as usual, with debt peonage, in effect, as great an evil as slavery. With a lack of incentives for both owners and peons, production was poor and Mexico failed to utilize new developments in agricultural machinery.

The burdens of the war fell heavily on the women of Mexico. When their men folk were conscripted into the army, the women carried on the work on the family farm, fighting plows through rough ground, planting and harvesting crops to feed their families, and selling produce at the markets to bring in a few pesos to clothe their children. While some hired out as laborers at the large plantations, many marched with their soldiers. These women continued the historic role of the soldaderas – the women warriors and auxiliaries who shared the hardships and the dangers of their men. The soldaderas were more than just camp followers. They foraged for food, carried supplies on their backs, nursed the wounded, and on some occasions fought alongside their men.

An example of their dedication was related by an American lieutenant during the fighting at Monterey. He wrote that in the middle of the fighting, he saw a soldadera carrying food and water to wounded men lying on the battlefield. The woman, he wrote, lifted the head of one groaning soldier, gave him water and then bandaged his wound with a scarf covering her head. Returning to her lines, she filled a pot with water and re-crossed the battlefield to help others. While in the line of fire, a stray bullet struck her and she fell dead.

While many soldiers, their women, and at Chapultepec even their children fought bravely, Mexico was a badly divided nation. The Mexican historian Lucas Alaman wrote in despair:

It seems reckless of Scott to march with such a small army against a city of 180,000 inhabitants plus a very considerable garrison, which outnumbers the attacking army ... despite this, there is no doubt in my mind that he will take the city ... Our army consists mainly of recruits under command of generals who are renowned for how fast they can flee, and nothing will move the masses, who are watching all this as if it were happening in a foreign country. That is how weary they are after so many revolts. This will all be over very soon.

Alaman's remarks were prophetic. A few days after the Americans occupied the capital and the street fighting ended, the gambling halls, saloons, cock fighting parlors, restaurants, coffee houses, and bordellos reopened with their proprietors greeting American soldiers and their dollars with welcoming smiles.

The Americans

When Polk was elected president, he vowed to do two things – acquire California and settle the Oregon boundaries. In order to accomplish the first, however, he had to resolve the second.

It was one thing to pressure Mexico into selling their north-western territory at the risk of war; it was another to risk fighting Great Britain and Canada over a dispute about the proper latitude of the Oregon Territory.

In August 1814, an American delegation led by John Quincy Adams met with their British counterparts in Ghent, Belgium, to settle what the Americans called the War of 1812. The treaty ended the fighting but left unresolved several problems, including the Oregon boundaries.

The British claimed sovereignty in Oregon because of the establishment of Hudson's Bay Trading Company posts in the area, with their headquarters in Vancouver. American claims rested on an American ship's voyage up the Columbia River in 1792 and Lewis and Clark's expedition, which had entered Oregon during the winter of 1805/6. In 1835, the American claim was bolstered when missionaries to the Indian tribes and other settlers began to pour into the country.

By the time of Polk's inauguration, the United States was in the throes of its mystical drive for 'Manifest Destiny.' A driving part of American jingoism was the cry of 'Fifty-four forty or fight' from those said to suffer from 'Oregon fever.' The slogan meant that the American northern boundary for Oregon must be set at 54 degrees 40 minutes north latitude, or war must ensue.

Such a boundary would have had to take in the Canadian port of Vancouver and extend as far north as Rupert Sound, in what is now British Columbia. This, Polk realized, was both ridiculous and unobtainable. In the past, all American presidents, starting with James Monroe in 1817, had agreed that a proper boundary should be set at 49 degrees north latitude. Polk blustered to assuage the militants, but in June 1846, the British government, uninterested in fighting a war over a faraway land of dubious value, sent a draft treaty to the American government agreeing to the 49 degree boundary.

By this time, the United States was at war with Mexico and Polk considered it expedient to concur with the British proposal. He immediately agreed to the treaty and the United States Senate ratified it on 18 June 1846. The United States was then free to continue its war with Mexico uninterrupted.

While the lure for land drove many west during the war years, it was a trip fraught with peril. Starvation, contaminated water, Indian attacks, burning heat in the desert and plains, and freezing cold in the mountains caused many shallow graves on the trails to California, Oregon, and Utah. But still they came.

In midwinter of 1846, members of the Church of Jesus Christ of Latter Day Saints, better known as Mormons, were driven from their settlements in Nauvoo, Illinois, by violent mobs who opposed their religious beliefs. Under the leadership of Brigham Young, the colony began a long trek across half the continent to their final refuge in the Utah Territory.

They established winter quarters near present-day Omaha, Nebraska. Although suffering from near starvation and a cholera epidemic that killed 600, they assembled a Mormon Battalion of 500 men who pledged to fight for the United States in the war with Mexico. The battalion marched to California but arrived too late to take part in the fighting.

When the winter weather eased in April 1847, the Mormons continued their westward march. Some traveled in covered wagons pulled by mules, but many pushed their belongings across the plains and mountains in handcarts. After a journey of more than three months, a vanguard of 150 men, women, and children arrived at the valley of the Great Salt Lake on 24 July 1847. Upon arrival, they began to dig the irrigation ditches to bring water to the arid prairie where they planted their first crops. Facing possible raids from roving Indian bands, Young wisely made the decision: 'It is better to feed the Indians than fight them.' His policy of friendship resulted in a rare peace between the two races.

When the desert began to bloom, Mormons by the thousands journeyed to their new haven, headquartered at the newly founded Salt Lake City. A catastrophe nearly overtook the settlement in 1848 when swarms of crickets descended into their valley and began to devour their ripening crops. Providentially, flocks of sea gulls arrived over the Salt Lake area and devoured the crickets, thus saving the crops and preventing the starvation of the settlers.

Other pioneers were not so fortunate. During the winter of 1847, the Donner Party, consisting of 84 men, women, and children heading for California, were trapped by heavy snows in the Sierra Nevada mountains. After heroic attempts at rescue, 40 members were saved. But westerners, although toughened by many trials, were horrified to learn that during weeks of near starvation, some of the party had sustained themselves by eating the bodies of their dead.

Another tragedy befell Marcus Whitman and his beautiful wife, Narcissa. A physician and a missionary, Whitman had established a mission and hospital in the Walla Walla Valley in Oregon. On their first trip to the area, Narcissa became the first American woman to cross the Rocky Mountains. Within a few years, Whitman's mission became an important way station for incoming immigrants since an American medical doctor was a rarity in the west. Unfortunately, European and American diseases were transmitted by the immigrants to neighboring Indians, who had no immunities to those ailments. Many Indians died of measles, smallpox, and other diseases, and Whitman was blamed for the deaths of the tribesmen. On 29 November 1847, a war party of the Cayuse tribe attacked Whitman's mission and massacred the doctor, his wife, and 12 other settlers.

The war with Mexico fiercely divided the American people. While the majority supported the war, a loud minority despised it, and their rancor filled the newspapers and the debates in the houses of Congress.

A newly elected congressional representative from Illinois, Abraham Lincoln, declared: 'The war with Mexico was unnecessarily and unconstitutionally commenced by the president.' Lincoln challenged Polk on the issue that American blood had been shed on American soil and implied that the American troops were the aggressors. He charged that Polk desired 'military glory ... that serpent's eye which charms to destroy ... I more than suspect that Polk is deeply conscious of being in the wrong and that he feels the blood of this war, like the blood of Abel, is crying to Heaven against him.'

However, like many critics of the war, Lincoln voted for an appropriations bill to support military operations. An Illinois newspaper responded to Lincoln's fulminations by branding him a 'second Benedict Arnold,' and Lincoln was defeated for reelection.

Comparing Lincoln to Arnold was perhaps the most vicious charge that could then be made against an American. General Arnold has been a trusted favorite of George Washington during the American Revolutionary War. In August 1780 he had turned traitor and attempted to turn over the American army's position at West Point to the British in exchange for money and a brigadier's commission in the British army. His act of treachery was discovered but he was able to escape to safety behind British lines.

Henry Clay, a former senator from Kentucky and unsuccessful candidate for president, often called the 'Great Pacificator' or the 'Great Compromiser' for his efforts to hold the Union together, spoke out forcefully: 'The Mexican war,' he said, 'is one of unnecessary and offensive aggression … Mexico is defending her firesides, her castles, and her altars, not we.'

Representative Alexander Stephens of Georgia, in a protest rare among Southerners, pronounced: 'The principle of waging war against a neighboring people to compel them to sell their country is not only dishonorable but disgraceful and infamous.'

President Polk responded to his critics by claiming they were prolonging the war and 'giving aid and comfort to the enemy,' and while American soldiers were fighting and dying in Mexico, congressional opposition like Lincoln, fearful of being labeled traitors, for the most part voted appropriations to sustain the war effort.

Polk was a Democrat, and upon his election held a majority of votes in the House of Representatives and the Senate. In 1848, however, the opposition Whig party and dissident Democrats, led by Representative David Wilmot of Pennsylvania, proposed an amendment to the military appropriations bill. This stated that neither slavery nor involuntary servitude would be permitted in any territory seized from Mexico. After acrimonious debate, the House passed it but the Senate killed it. It had, however, resurrected again the issue of slavery, which began to permeate every facet of American political discussion.

One of the ironies in American political history occurred during the presidential election of 1848, when the Whigs, who had opposed the war, nominated General Zachary Taylor as their candidate.

The fevered political debates during the war years were fueled by major advances in publishing. New improvements in printing presses and paper manufacturing enabled publishers to produce newspapers, magazines, and books faster and in greater quantities than ever before. The American public, with one of the highest literacy rates in the world, hungered for news, and newspaper war correspondents satiated them with timely reports from the battlefields. As soon as correspondents or their messengers could reach the newly developed telegraph lines, their words could be sent quickly throughout the country. The big steam-powered presses enabled magazine and book publishers to flood the markets with cheap publications featuring tales of the military exploits of home-town soldiers, as well as fictional accounts of the fighting.

The war years did not, however, have much influence on the development of American literature. The only major writer who wrote a war novel was James Fenimore Cooper, and poets John Greenleaf Whittier and James Russell Lowell denounced the war in forgettable poetry and prose.

Perhaps the most important literary influence on the American thirst for California was written by a young American sailor, Richard Henry Dana Jr. While a student at Harvard, Dana traveled to the Pacific and then spent a year working in California. His book *Two Years Before the Mast*, published in 1840, provided an exhilarating picture of San Francisco Bay. He described the bay and the surrounding lands in their pristine state, unspoiled by the commerce of men but inviting in its splendid harbor, its beautiful birds, and its plentiful game.

Another literary work initiated during the war years was the journey of historian Francis Parkman, who set out in 1846 for the Oregon Territory. In his magisterial work *The Oregon Trail*, published in 1849, he chronicled his adventures on the trail from St. Louis to the Pacific Ocean. Parkman described the dangers, the hardships, and the loneliness of travel through the vast spaces of the west. He foretold the passing of the buffalo and the corralling of the nomadic Indian tribes as the swarming numbers of covered wagons continued to broaden the western trails and thousands of new settlers began to fill up the pristine lands.

The war years heralded a major development in medicine, when in October 1846, anesthesia was first used to relieve pain during surgery. The pain killer letheon was administered to a soldier whose legs were amputated after they were crushed in an accident. While the pain reliever was a godsend to badly wounded soldiers, many still continued to die as a result of infections and the always lethal gangrene. The most deadly killer was still diarrhoea, which was not well understood by physicians of the day. It was often treated with ineffective medicines or by the almost medieval concept of bleeding the patient every few days.

While more than 100,000 men served in the military during the war, the American economy was not strained by the war effort. With a population of more than 20 million, constantly increased by swarms of European immigrants, the absence of the men in uniform was hardly noticed, except by family and friends.

Unlike the women of Mexico, American women were not thrust into men's jobs in order to provide for their families. During the 1840s and for several generations thereafter, American women's activities centered around home and family. Some were required to manage family farms while their husbands were serving in Mexico, but large families and an abundance of labor eased the absence.

Many women, usually those with family members in the ranks, volunteered to sew bandages, blankets, socks, and other wearable items for their loved ones. Others – abolitionists or those who opposed the war on religious or humanitarian grounds – spoke out against it, though dissenting voices were few.

At first, the American war effort faced financial difficulties. In 1842, the government, in an effort to protect growing American industries and, as Southerners would say, to force them to buy eastern goods, set a high tariff on imports. While the tariff was successful in stifling foreign competition, it also drastically reduced government revenues and put severe limitations on the extension of international credit to American entrepreneurs. Coupled with currency inflation and a slowing of the business cycle, the United States Treasury was hard put to finance a war.

At the beginning of hostilities, the treasury held only a small surplus of $7 million. When Polk recommended that the Congress place additional taxes on coffee and tea, the House of Representatives indignantly refused. Polk, however, was able to have passed a new bill lowering tariffs, and by the beginning of 1847 revenues began to increase. The Congress also voted to issue $10 million in new Treasury notes and bonds.

Technical advances in agriculture increased production when, in 1846, John Deere constructed the first plow with a steel moldboard. The American agricultural picture brightened in 1847 when famine in Ireland and Germany resulted in an increased sale of American grain and corn. As additional revenues flowed in from increased foreign trade and American victories on the battlefield became known, European credit restrictions loosened. As a result the American economy rebounded and entered a period of increased prosperity.

Europe

While the war between the United States and Mexico raged, across the Atlantic, Europe was in the throes of epochal changes in

industry, politics, science, religion, and the arts. This vast ferment of new ideas was brought about by a combination of factors, including the Industrial Revolution, the French and American revolutions, scientific discoveries, and democratic ideals.

Throughout the continent machines were replacing craftsmen, and home shops were being replaced by large factories employing thousands. There was a rush to the cities as population growth created surplus farm laborers. The new capitalism spawned a society based on competitive enterprise producing large numbers of goods made by machinery operated by poorly paid workers. While cheap goods were beneficial to many, workers often lived in slums, and children were pushed into the maw of industrial production lines.

With the creation of more wealth, the expansion of education, and the

Expanding railroads began stretching across both Europe and the United States, creating a revolution in land transportation at the dawning of the industrial age. Other significant developments were John Deere's plow, featuring a steel moldboard, and Elias Howe's patent for the first practical sewing machine. (Ann Ronan Picture Library)

proliferation of newspapers, magazines, and books, an influential group of intellectuals and writers arose who determined to change the human condition. Middle-class liberalism, businessmen frustrated by the privileges and power of the nobility, and romantic intellectualism, coupled with the workers' poverty, alienation, and hostility, formed a heady brew of opposition to the status quo.

In 1848 these resentments came to a head and revolts broke out all over Europe. Revolutionists in Paris overthrew the Orleans monarchy, driving King Louis Philippe from

Grand symphony orchestras, ballets, and large choral groups playing the romantic works of European composers enthralled audiences during the mid-nineteenth century. Berlioz's *Damnation of Faust*, Mendelssohn's *Elijah*, and Verdi's *Macbeth* thrilled elite audiences in grand concert halls. (Ann Ronan Picture Library)

the throne and establishing the Second Republic. In Austria, Prince Metternich, a strong supporter of autocracy and police despotism who strived to suppress constitutional and popular democracy, was forced to flee the country. North Italy and Hungary fought the French, the Poles fought the Germans, and an insurrection raged in Prague. Other outbreaks threatened to overturn governments in Venice, Berlin, and Milan, while Republican rebels forced the Pope to flee Rome.

While these revolts were bloodily repulsed by the established order, they led to a continued tension between worker and capitalist, serf and landowner, and democrat and royalist. In 1848, Karl Marx published the *Communist Manifesto*: 'Workers of the world unite, you have nothing to lose but your chains.' It became a cry for the working class to overturn the entire social, economic, and political structures of Europe.

During the same year, John Stuart Mill, the English philosopher, social reformer, and economist, wrote *Principles of Political Economy*. Later, he was to write a series of works in which he eloquently defended the freedoms of the individual in opposition to the social and political controls of governments. Mill believed that the individual ought to be able to do or say anything as long as it did not harm others.

By 1840, Charles Darwin, the English naturalist whose theories would cause a revolution in both scientific and religious worlds, had returned from his sea voyages and was busily writing of his discoveries. In 1846, he published several works on his geological and zoological findings from his voyages in the Pacific. They were to be the forerunners to his explosive *On the Origin of Species*, which was to shake both science

and fundamental religious foundations throughout the world.

In Europe and America, the war years were a time of dynamic change, while Mexico stagnated, struggling only for survival.

Under the growing impact of the factory economy, poverty and industrial abuse were causing increasing unrest among workers. In 1848, Karl Marx and Frederick Engels completed their *Communist Manifesto*. It was to be a harbinger of great struggles to come. (Ann Ronan Picture Library)

Mary Ann Maverick:
A Texas pioneer

Mary Ann Adams was born on a prosperous plantation in Tuskaloosa County, Alabama, on 16 March 1818. When she was 18 years old she met Samuel Maverick, a rugged adventurer from Texas, and it was love at first sight. On 4 August 1836, Mary married the handsome 33-year-old Texan in a ceremony at her widowed mother's plantation.

Maverick, born in South Carolina, came from a distinguished family who had sent him east to school. He received a degree from Yale University, studied law, and was admitted to the South Carolina Bar. In 1835, caught up in the lure of Texas, he joined their revolutionary army and became a signer of the Texas Declaration of Independence. After capture and then escape from a Mexican prison, Maverick traveled to Alabama on business where he met the vivacious Mary.

After the ceremony, they visited relatives in Alabama and Louisiana. When Mary became pregnant, they stayed at the Maverick plantation in South Carolina until the birth of their first son, on 14 May 1837. On 14 October, they set off on an epic journey to the new Republic of Texas. Their entourage included Sam, Mary, infant Sam, Mary's 15-year-old brother, Robert, and 10 Negro slaves.

Journeying to savage Texas in the 1830s was, to most, a trip to the ends of the earth, and Mary recounted her mother sobbing: 'Oh, Mary, I will never see you again on earth.' Sam drove a carriage for his wife and five-month-old son; the others piled into a large wagon or walked. Tied behind the wagon were 'three saddle horses and one blooded filly' according to a diary Mary kept throughout her life.

Their big wagon carried a tent, bedding, cooking utensils, and food. Mary wrote that most of the trip was 'delightful' as the little caravan stopped several days at a time to rest, cook, and wash, and 'sometimes to give muddy roads time to dry.'

After trekking more than 400 miles, they crossed the muddy Sabine River and entered Texas on New Year's Day 1838. Heading west for San Antonio, on 26 January, Mary wrote: 'We entered a bleak, desolate, swamp-prairie cut by deep gullies.' Knee-deep in water, they 'stalled in five or six gullies and each time the wagon had to be unloaded.' After straining to get to dry ground, they reloaded the wagon and pushed on until they were again stopped by deep water and mud. Then they repeated the process.

It took them four days to cross the 14 miles of swamp, and during that time Mary experienced her first Texas 'norther.' It was, she wrote, 'a terrific howling north wind with a fine rain penetrating through clothes and blankets. Never in my life had I felt such cold.' Their provisions were almost exhausted when on 30 January they reached the small settlement of Navidad. Continuing on, two of their horses froze to death during another norther. The final leg of the trek was uneventful except for a broken wagon-wheel which was mended with rawhide.

While on the trail, on 8 June, they were visited by a war band of 17 Tonkawa Indians who proudly displayed two scalps, one hand, and 'several pieces of putrid flesh from various parts of the human body which were being taken to their squaws to eat.' Sam, Robert, and four of the male servants nervously fondled rifles and pistols while Mary sat on the wagon seat with her 'pistol and Bowie knife visible' and made small talk with the Indians. Mary wrote: 'I was frightened almost to death, but tried not to show my alarm.' The Indians apparently decided the well-armed Mavericks would be too tough to assault and rode away grumbling.

On 15 June 1837, the Mavericks drove into the main plaza of San Antonio and found themselves in a small but lovely city, where the San Antonio River with its sparkling, clear spring waters ran through the middle of the settlement. Its banks were

Mary A. Maverick was the paradigm of the pioneer woman of the Texas frontier. Born in Alabama, she married Samuel Maverick, a prominent lawyer and politician, and journeyed to San Antonio in the Texas settlements in 1836. Her memoirs give one of the most engrossing and colorful accounts of life on the wild frontier. (Courtesy of the Maverick family)

Sam Maverick bought this plain but spacious house in Alamo Plaza in San Antonio. He chose that site so that he could view the Alamo Mission, where many of his close friends, both Texans and Mexicans, had been killed in the siege in 1836. (Courtesy of the Maverick family)

shaded with post oak, cypress, and pecan trees, and flowers bloomed in the dooryards of the Canary Islanders who had settled in the city in 1731.

Earlier, in 1718, Spaniards had established the Mission San Antonio de Valero, later called the *Alamo*, the Mexican-Spanish word for cottonwood tree. The name was derived from the cottonwood trees growing in abundance around its walls. The city slumbered lazily in the Texas sun until the 1820s, when the Spanish government encouraged settlement by Americans. In 1824, Mexico ousted the Spaniards, but its reign lasted less than 12 years. In 1836, American settlers and local Mexicans rose up in revolt and won their independence after fierce fighting.

When the Mavericks arrived, the city had already begun to take on a cosmopolitan air. On a typical day, mingling in the plaza before the majestic San Fernando Cathedral,

couples with surnames like Navarro, Seguin, and Guerrero along with Campbell, Adams, and McCutchon could be found; soon Germans with names like Wurzbach, Guenther, and Altgelt also became prominent in city affairs.

Sam's law practice flourished and he was soon elected to the Texas Congress. On 19 January 1839, the Mavericks purchased a stone house on the city's main plaza. From their front porch, Sam and Mary could see the battered remains of the Alamo, where Crockett, Bowie, Travis, and 150 other Texans had fought to the last man.

In their back yard Mary had a garden that boasted 16 large fig trees and rows of pomegranates. She was able to enjoy music and singing after a neighbor managed to transport an ancient piano to San Antonio. Another neighbor sold her milk at 25 cents a gallon, chickens at 12 cents apiece, and pumpkins at 25 cents. On 23 March 1839, her second son was born.

On the outskirts of San Antonio all was not serene. Comanche raiders and Mexican bandits roamed the countryside stealing stock and waylaying unwary or unarmed travelers. When a raid was reported, the church bells at the cathedral would be rung and volunteers, including Sam, would grab their guns, mount their horses and pursue the raiders. If they caught them, it was a battle to the death. The Texans did not take prisoners. The Comanches did, often for the pleasure of torturing them to death.

In 1840, Comanches asking for a parley entered San Antonio, but the peace talks soon degenerated into a wild running fight. Mary wrote that when the clash started she ran to her house, beating two pursuing Indians to her door by a hair's breadth. Hearing the commotion, Sam grabbed his rifle and rushed into the street, but in the back yard three Comanches were about to attack Mary's Negro cook and her two children. The cook, unfazed, waved a large rock in her hand and screamed that she would bash in the skull of any Indian that approached.

The Indians backed away and then ran for the nearby San Antonio River. Mary's brother, Andrew, dashed from the house and shot and killed one Indian as he ran down the bank. Another Comanche made it to the opposite bank, but Andrew dropped him with another shot. While the fighting raged on, Mary went out her front door and found a dying Indian lying by her front gate. Two others lay dead in the street. After the fleeing Comanches escaped from the city and returned to their camp, Mary learned they 'roasted and butchered' their 13 American captives in revenge.

In March 1842, when scouts warned that an invading Mexican army was approaching, the Mavericks and a dozen other Anglo families fled. They loaded tents and provisions into a cart, buried some valuables under the floor of their house, and headed east. Mary sometimes rode beside Sam but other times she drove the cart, nestling their five-month-old baby daughter in her lap.

There followed a five-year exile from their home. The small caravan wandered through the countryside until 21 June, when they settled in La Grange in east Texas.

Sam had returned to San Antonio in the late summer of 1842 when a second invasion struck in September. Sam and 50 Anglos put up a stiff fight against a force of 1,400 Mexican regulars until they were forced to surrender. He and other leading citizens were then marched 1,200 miles into Mexico and thrown into Perote prison near Mexico City.

Mary, in the meantime, had moved into a log cabin with her three children. She made ends meet with 20 gold doubloons Sam had managed to smuggle to her via a friend. It was a terrible time. Mary wrote: 'I strove to be brave and prayed to God that I might live for my children and my dear husband.'

A month before Sam was released, in April 1843, and rejoined his family, Mary gave birth to her second daughter. In 1844, Sam and Mary decided to move to Matagorda Peninsula to take advantage of the more balmy Gulf Coast climate. There, Mary grew watermelons and flowers, and planted orange trees and grape vines.

In 1847, after the annexation of Texas by the United States and once fears of Mexican invasion had ended and the Comanches had become less of a menace, the Mavericks returned to San Antonio. They arrived in October and found the town booming as a result of American and German immigrants swarming into Texas. Their old home was battered but sound, although the garden was a wreck. Happily, the fig trees were still bearing fruit.

In May 1848, Mary's eight-year-old daughter Agatha died of fever. In 1880, Mary wrote: 'After thirty-two years, I cannot dwell on that terrible bereavement." It got worse: a year later, in April 1849, cholera struck San Antonio and her daughter Augusta died in the epidemic.

As the frontier receded, the Mavericks began a less hectic but more prosperous life. Mary gave birth, in all, to 10 children, although her last child, a daughter, died before reaching her second birthday.

Sam Maverick died in 1870, but Mary lived until 1898. Exciting though her early life was, it was not at all unusual for a Texas pioneer.

The Halls of Montezuma

Scott's decision to attack Chapultepec was not greeted with great enthusiasm by his army. The frontal attacks at Molino del Rey had caused heavy casualties, and because Scott's clever flanking attacks during most of the earlier battles had produced victories with a low butcher's bill, his officers studied the approaches to Mexico City with dismay.

Between the causeways leading to the city were deep marshes, where much of the land was under water. It would be difficult for infantry and cavalry, but impossible for artillery to cross these areas. The only feasible routes were along the elevated causeways, which were sure to be swept with heavy artillery and infantry fire. To enter the city there seemed to be no choice but to launch costly frontal attacks.

After studying the results of Lee's reconnaissance, Scott determined that he must attack along the San Cosme Causeway on the west and at the Belen Causeway to the south-west of Chapultepec Castle. The castle soared a rocky 200 feet above the marshes and its summit was lined with heavy brick and stone buildings. These housed the Mexican military academy and the summer palace formerly used by the Spanish viceroy.

Defending the position were more than 2,000 soldiers and the cadet corps of the military academy. The infantry was backed up by more than a dozen cannon emplaced along the ramparts. The Americans would have to climb up the rocky hill and scale the walls of the castle without cover and under constant fire.

The army's dismay turned to fury when they learned that after Mexican attackers at the Molino had overrun an American unit, they had cut the throats of helpless wounded soldiers. Grim-faced, the Americans muttered 'No prisoners' during the attack on the castle.

At dawn on 12 September, the American artillery began a thunderous barrage on the Mexican defenders. The following morning, Scott ordered a general attack.

Brigadier General Gideon Pillow's division, attacking from the west, was the first to fight its way to the castle walls, but their cheers turned to curses when they realized that some idiot of a quartermaster had failed to bring up the scaling ladders.

Huddling against the walls, they waited for what seemed an eternity until the ladders were brought up. Then, under covering fire from the artillery, they climbed up to the parapets and fought their way over the wall in bloody close combat. Among the assaulting troops were 40 United States

Pillow's Division launched a wild charge on the westward defenses of Chapultepec, racing through a torrent of grapeshot and musket balls. When a flag bearer was shot down, Lieutenant George Pickett, fresh out of West Point, picked up the flag and led his screaming men to the castle battlements. Climbing up scaling ladders, they fought with rifle butts and bayonets to drive the defenders from the walls. (Painting by Carl Nebel, Archives Division, Texas State Library)

Marines. Their heroics led to the opening lines of the Marine Corps Hymn – 'From the Halls of Montezuma ... we will fight our country's battles on land and on the sea.'

As the Americans advanced through the castle, there occurred a defining event in the history of the Mexican people. Fighting alongside the Mexican soldiers were 50 teenaged military school cadets, some as young as 13, who refused to retreat before the swarming Americans. When the surging Americans rushed at one 13-year-old cadet, he refused to throw down his musket and surrender. He was quickly bayoneted. Three other cadets, fighting like demons, were killed in the palace corridors, while another was shot to death on the school grounds.

Another young cadet was stationed on the palace roof, defending the flagstaff from which the torn and shot-holed Mexican flag still flew. As the invading troops charged up the stairway to the roof, the young lad,

refusing to see his country's colors captured, hauled down the flag. As he dashed along the parapet, his body was ripped by bullets. Wrapped in his country's flag, he fell to the rocks below. More than a century and a half later, this story is still recounted to every Mexican schoolchild. Today, at the foot of Chapultepec there is a large monument, sacred to all Mexicans, honoring *Los Niños Heroicos*.

Within less than two hours of hard fighting the Stars and Stripes was flying boldly from the Chapultepec battlements. The Americans had lost another 500 men

BELOW When Quitman's troops breached the southern defenses of Chapultepec after suffering heavy losses, they joined up with Pillow's assault troops. The tough, heroic, but doomed defenders broke, and the survivors fled north to Mexico City. Quitman's troops, in hot pursuit, advanced to the city gates but were recalled by Scott. (Painting by Carl Nebel, Archives Division, Texas State Library)

ABOVE On 14 September 1848, General Winfield Scott and his staff rode into the Zocalo, the main plaza of Mexico City, while a military band played *Yankee Doodle*. As the Stars and Stripes fluttered in a soft breeze from the National Palace, Scott, saluting, reviewed his ragged but victorious troops. (Painting by Carl Nebel, Archives Division, Texas State Library)

from their thinning ranks; the Mexicans had suffered more than 1,500 casualties.

The American attacks continued to push toward the center of Mexico City. Shortly before noon, Quitman's men took the Belen Gate by storm. General Worth's troops were before the San Cosme Gate by 4.00pm but encountered fierce resistance. Burrowing through the adobe houses along the causeway, and with assistance from Lieutenant Grant and his howitzer, they broke through the gate by suppertime. On the night of 13 September, the exhausted Americans held the keys to the capital.

Before dawn on 14 September, a Mexican delegation waving a white flag approached General Quitman's division and surrendered the city. At first light, American troops moved into the main plaza and raised their flag. An hour later, Scott, wearing his best dress uniform, and his staff rode proudly into the plaza. As he passed in review of his ragged, grimy veterans, with six months of brutal fighting behind them, they rent the air with chorus after chorus of cheers.

The fighting, however, was not yet ended. Fuming with hatred of the invader, hundreds of citizens of the capital sniped at the Americans from rooftops or otherwise clashed with the troops in three days of violence. Much of the trouble began when Santa Anna, in a moment of spite, released several

The Mexican War battles saw bitter hand-to-hand fighting resulting in heavy casualties being suffered by both sides. (San Jacinto Museum of History Association)

thousand criminals from the city's jails. It was they who indiscriminately plundered civilian houses throughout the city.

Scott decreed martial law. His troops tore through houses believed to harbor snipers and rooftops were cleared with blasts of canister. Patrols had soon rounded up the criminals and returned them to their cells, and by 16 September, although the hatred remained, the fighting had died down.

Santa Anna, who had urged his compatriots to fight to the death, had no such intentions for himself. Early in the battle, he and his remaining troops scampered north to the town of Guadalupe Hidalgo. On 18 September, he wrote a bombastic

pronunciamento blaming his generals for the defeats and falsely claiming that he had been in the thick of the fighting with American bullets piercing his clothing. He was resigning the presidency, he said, in order to personally lead his troops 'in the quarter in which there is the most peril.' With that, the 'Napoleon of the West' marched his remaining troops south-east and conducted a half-hearted siege of Puebla, occupied by a small American garrison. On 1 October, he gave up the siege. A new government relieved him of command and later banished him from the country. He took refuge, temporarily, in Jamaica.

When the fighting with the Mexicans ended, the American leaders were free to

Nicholas P. Trist, sent to negotiate a peace treaty with Mexico, was recalled by Polk. Ignoring orders, Trist signed the Treaty of Guadalupe Hidalgo which ended the war. (Library of Congress)

indulge in political battles against each other. Scott had Generals Worth and Pillow placed under arrest for insubordination, claiming they had circulated stories giving themselves, not Scott, responsibility for winning the battles. Scott's action enraged President Polk, a political ally of both generals, and he ordered them released. Three months later, on 13 January 1848, Polk relieved Scott of command and the general returned unheralded to the United States that spring.

The diplomatic front was no less chaotic. Earlier, in October 1847, Polk had recalled his peace negotiator, Nicolas P. Trist. However, Trist did not receive the order until the end of that year, and when he did, he ignored the President and continued attempts to secure a peace treaty. Following entreaties from Trist, Polk allowed him to continue negotiations. After long months of haggling the Mexicans finally gave in, and on 2 February 1848, they reluctantly signed the Treaty of Guadalupe Hidalgo.

The Mexicans hated the treaty's provisions, while some of the more hawkish Americans, who wanted to annex all of Mexico, opposed it. Polk, however, approved it as negotiated by Trist and his wishes prevailed.

The treaty was ratified on 10 March by the United States Senate and by the Mexican government on 25 March. The American war with Mexico was finally over. Polk, who hated Trist, recalled his envoy to Washington, D.C., dismissed him from the State Department, and refused to pay his expenses from Mexico.

The last American troops sailed from Mexico in August 1848. Neither country would ever be the same again. It was a war the Mexicans would long remember and the Americans would like to conveniently forget.

Trist shocked Mexican negotiators with his demands for Mexican territory. But their armies routed and their country racked with political unrest, they reluctantly surrendered more than half of their country. (Library of Congress)

RIGHT TOP On 12 September, American artillery launched a day-long bombardment on the fortified heights of Chapultepec Castle, which guarded Mexico City. When dawn broke, the Americans made a three-pronged attack on the more gradual slopes on the west and south sides of the castle.
Pillow and Worth on the west attacked under heavy fire, while Quitman's attack from the south along the Tacubaya Causeway was stalled by tough defenders. Swinging to their left, Quitman's troops braved intense enemy fire to place ladders against the walls and fight their way into the castle, linking up with Pillow and Worth's men who had also broken through. The Mexican defense collapsed and the Americans swarmed into the castle. The way to Mexico City was open, and by 14 September, Scott and his tough little army were camped on the main plaza in Mexico City.

RIGHT BOTTOM With the Oregon Territory dispute settled and American armies in possession of California, the United States spanned the North American continent from the Atlantic to the Pacific. The Mexican government was forced to sign the Treaty of Guadalupe Hidalgo on 10 March 1848. Including Texas, the Mexicans had surrendered more than 1,200,000 square miles to the United States. Within a few decades, the vast empty spaces of these rich lands would swarm with peoples from all over the globe.

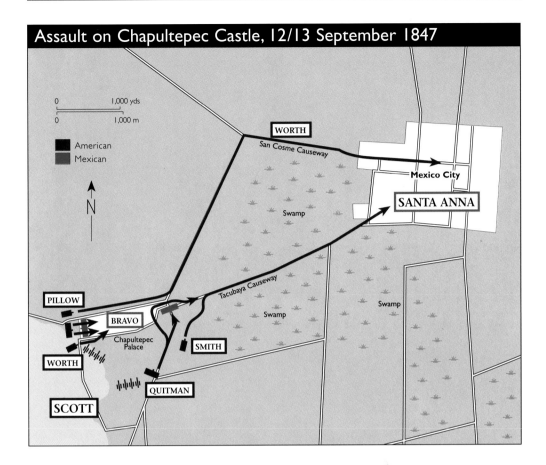

Assault on Chapultepec Castle, 12/13 September 1847

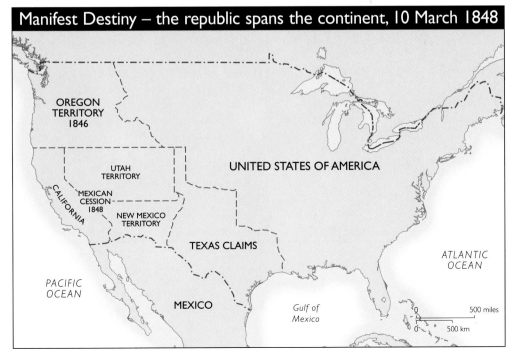

Manifest Destiny – the republic spans the continent, 10 March 1848

A new Colossus is born

At the conclusion of the war, Mexico was literally a broken nation. Her armies had been shattered in combat, with battle losses estimated at between 12,000 and 15,000, and many more who had deserted. Several of her major cities had had their most productive industries smashed into rubble, their foreign markets and imports had been destroyed, transportation was disrupted, and hunger was rampant. It has been estimated that disease, starvation, and dislocation caused thousands of civilian deaths during the war years.

The northern half of Mexican territory was sheared off by the harsh Treaty of Guadalupe Hidalgo. Including Texas, the United States acquired what was to become the states of New Mexico, Arizona, California, Nevada, Utah, and parts of Wyoming and Colorado.

The United States acquired more than 500,000 square miles of Mexican territory. If Texan territorial claims are counted, the total amount of land torn from Mexico exceeded one million square miles. With it went the vast mineral resources of the western states as well as the agricultural wealth of California.

The new boundary between the two countries would stretch from the mouth of the Rio Grande River on the Gulf of Mexico to the point where the river turns north at El Paso del Norte. From there, it would follow a westerly direction until it reached the Pacific Ocean.

In compensation, the United States would pay the Mexican government $15 million; it would also pay to Americans the $3.25 million in claims they held against Mexico; and Mexicans living in the United States would be eligible to become American citizens. A further condition, never effectively enforced, provided that the American army would guard the border and prevent attacks into Mexico from predatory Indian tribes living on US territory.

Aghast at this dismemberment of their country, following what they considered 'The most unjust war in the history of the world,' many Mexicans demanded of their government: 'Give us arms and we will fight on.'

The *Criollos* or *Creoles* (Whites of Spanish descent born in Mexico), who dominated the upper echelons of the Mexican government, however, reluctantly accepted the treaty. They feared that continued fighting would disrupt what was left of the shattered Mexican polity, leading to another revolution in which caste and class would be pitted against one another in a bloodbath. Better to give up half of Mexico, the Creoles reasoned, than to have their heads stuck on a pikestaff in a city square. They may, indeed, have saved their necks, but the acceptance of the treaty sounded the death knell of the Criollo oligarchy.

Among those who supported the peace treaty were the bishops of the Catholic Church. They feared that their vast properties would be heavily taxed or their assets seized during a prolonged war. The British government, aware that the Americans were planning to pay Mexico a huge indemnity, also urged peace. British support rested not on altruism, however, but rather on hopes that a bonanza of dollars would enable the Mexicans to pay the massive debts to British holders of Mexican bonds which had been outstanding for more than 20 years.

With Mexico in political crisis, Santa Anna was called back from exile and on 20 April 1853, he again assumed the presidency. Strapped for cash, on 30 December 1853, he sold 29,640 square miles of Mexican land bordering New Mexico and Arizona to the United States for $10 million. The Gadsden Purchase, named after James Gadsden, the American agent who arranged the deal, gave the Americans a route for a proposed railway linking the east with the west coast. Outraged Mexicans, however, again threw Santa Anna out of office and into exile.

Santa Anna mirrored the cynicism of the day when he remarked that it would be 100 years before his people would be fit for self-government. Only despots like himself, he contended, could bring stability to Mexico. During the decade of the 1840s, while Europe was undergoing huge change, and often convulsions, in economic, social, religious, and political philosophies, Mexico stagnated in a pond of cynicism and despair.

During 1848, in the Yucatán, the War of the Castes broke out, pitting Mayan Indians against Spaniards and Mestizos in an orgy of brutality. The Mexicans shot their opponents without remorse, while the Indians gang-raped women and skinned alive male captives or turned them into flaming torches. The violence spread to the center of Mexico. Agrarian revolts against the hacienda owners created destruction and terror as the victims of debt peonage rose up with the cry 'Death to the *Gachupines*' (European-born Spaniards).

To make matters worse, the Apaches of New Mexico and Arizona and the Comanches of north Texas made devastating raids into the northern states of Sonora, Chihuahua, Coahuila, and Tamaulipas, practically depopulating many towns and agricultural settlements. Dodging American army patrols, Indian war parties crossed into Mexico to steal cattle, horses, grain, and other foodstuffs, to butcher the inhabitants and then retreat into the haven of the United States.

Bankrupt, economically ruined, divided by race, language, and stratified social classes, Mexico sank into a dark age. The misery, however, bred reform. Mexicans, shocked at the conditions in their country, demanded change. Many blamed the residue of Spanish colonialism for their troubles. The aristocratic Creole officers who could strut but not fight, and the Church hierarchy who were more interested in protecting their property than in preserving their country were the causes of Mexican disasters, according to the reformers.

Writers, artists, composers and other intellectuals led the way, in a movement that threw off many of the cultural shackles of Europe. Secular in outlook and anti-military, many reached back into their pre-Cortez heritage to find a Mexico rooted in its distant past. Blending both their Indian and Spanish heritage, they created a culture that was distinctively Mexican. From this emerged a revitalized literature, a distinctive music, and the bright and flamboyant use of color and imagery that characterizes Mexican art.

Sadly, political progress did not keep pace with the artistic. Mexico was divided by a contest between liberals and conservatives. The liberals supported radical change to democratize, secularize, and industrialize Mexico in order to forge a united nation from the diverse class, caste, race, and linguistic differences that had traditionally divided the country. The conservatives, while supporting many of the nationalistic ideas of the liberals, feared that much of the liberal program would lead to further peasant and Indian uprisings. They believed that participation in the government by ordinary people should be restricted and that the Church and the military, both pillars of stability, must flourish and be supported by the government.

Unable to reconcile these divergent views, Mexicans engaged in yet another cycle of protracted violence. Less than two decades after the American war, a Zapotec Indian would clash with an Austrian-born emperor supported by a French army for the domination of Mexico. Benito Juarez, the Indian, became the liberal president of Mexico; and Emperor Ferdinand-Joseph Maximilian ended his reign before a Mexican firing squad.

In all this there seemed only two things that all Mexicans could all agree upon: they suffered a sickness of the soul for their fragmented country and they held a fear of and loathing for 'The Colossus of the North.'

At the conclusion of the war with Mexico, the United States bestrode the North American continent with one leg anchored on the Atlantic seaboard and the other on the Pacific. It was the fulfilment of their 'Manifest Destiny,' which proclaimed that the United States was ordained by God to stretch from 'sea to shining sea.' If the expansion of this republic was destined to be delivered in blood, the soldiers of Generals Taylor and Scott had paid in full. Of the small American armies, more than 13,000 had left their bones in Mexico, some through combat but many more through disease; another 4,000 had been wounded.

The war cost the American government almost $100 million, a massive fortune in those days. However, it was soon recovered because nine days after the Treaty of Guadalupe Hidalgo was signed, American prospectors struck gold in California. During the first decade of the California Gold Rush, the state produced quantities of the precious metal valued at more than $500 million.

The discovery of gold set off a flood of emigrants seeking their fortunes in the west. By the end of 1849, the population of California had swelled to more than 125,000 settlers.

There was also a massive exodus from Europe to the United States. Most were famine-fleeing Irish peasants and idealistic Germans searching for a life free of the strutting little monarchies of Central Europe. The liberal political uprisings in Europe beginning in 1848 sent another wave of immigrants to America.

One inducement for immigration was the high wages paid in America to both industrial and agricultural workers. European journalists reported that not only were wages much higher than in Europe, but they were high enough for a family to save. One Irishman wrote that if a man was gainfully employed, he could save enough money each week to purchase an acre and a half of 'the finest land in the world.' In less than a year of steady work, he wrote, a man could save enough money to head west and buy an 80-acre farm, on which he and his family could live forever.

One element of what was to become the American Dream was the growth of free public schools. It became an axiom of Americans, old and new, that with education and hard work any person could transcend the poverty of his birth and rise to the highest status of society in the land.

If in Europe there was political ferment, in the United States the political winds of change were also blowing. During the presidential election of 1844, President Polk had pledged himself to a single term of office. Broken in health from the strains of his presidency, he kept his promise and retired to private life. In the scramble for succession General Zachary Taylor defeated Winfield Scott for the Whig party nomination and then went on to win the presidency. His campaign was based on his military prowess and ignored the looming conflict over slavery. Taylor found it expedient to avoid the slavery question since, as a Louisiana plantation owner, he owned scores of slaves. After only a few months in office, however, Taylor died of typhus fever, leaving the office to the nonentity Millard Fillmore, who did nothing to quell the growing rupture between the industrializing east and the agricultural, slave-holding Southern states.

In the 1852 presidential election, Winfield Scott finally secured the Whig nomination, only to be defeated by the Democratic Party nominee, Franklin Pierce, a former general of volunteers in the Mexican War who had served under Scott.

Most eastern intellectuals had opposed the war. They considered it as nothing but a land grab, sponsored by the Southern states as a means of extending slavery. This was, of course, a fallacy, because the western lands were not climatically suitable for growing tobacco or cotton, the South's major export crops. Nevertheless, distrust between the Northern and Southern states increased after the cessation of hostilities with Mexico.

As the northern, eastern and western states in the Union exploded with new industries, expanding transportation facilities and rapidly increasing population, the South slumbered. Slave-ridden and agricultural, the Southern states slept in the sun. Its elite viewed themselves more as romantic paladins out of the novels of Sir Walter Scott; their eastern neighbors emulated the heroes of Horatio Alger, a clergyman who had written more than 100 children's books in which poverty-stricken street boys rose by hard work and business acumen to positions of wealth and influence.

As the ideals of Jeffersonian democracy clashed with the 'peculiar institution' of slavery, the North and the South moved toward irrepressible conflict. Most notable in opposition to the war with Mexico was Henry David Thoreau. He had refused to pay taxes to 'support an unjust government waging an unjust war.' Thoreau chronicled his opposition in his famous writings *Civil Disobedience*, in which he stated that the supremacy of the conscience of the individual was superior to the dictates of the government. 'Under a government which imprisons unjustly,' he wrote, 'the true place for a just man is also in prison.' Predictably, he was accommodated and was confined for a brief time in a cell. His writings, however, set the stage for future philosophical and political dissenters who used nonviolent methods to oppose their governments. Notable persons influenced by Thoreau included Mohandas K. Gandhi and Martin Luther King Jr.

During the postwar years, in seemingly endless debates the Congress moved away from efforts to compromise the differences between the free and the slave states and toward a fierce confrontation. Northern abolitionists believed the Congress had the right to enact legislation that would ban slavery, particularly in the newly acquired territories. The South countered with the proposition that Congress did not have the authority to ban slavery anywhere. Moreover, they maintained, it was the constitutional duty of the Congress and the federal government to protect the 'peculiar institution' of slavery. And with an edict that enraged abolitionists, they demanded that fugitive slaves who had fled and reached a haven in the North must be arrested and returned to their masters.

The jockeying for control of the United States Senate (where each state, regardless of size and population, had only two votes) ended when, in the fall of 1850, the territory of California entered the Union as a free state. Soon after, Minnesota and Oregon joined the Union as free states. These acts insured that in the future the United States Congress would be controlled in both houses by antislavery free states.

The South, seeing itself destined to be outvoted on every issue, began to seek relief in the idea of separation from the Union. Their great champion, Senator John C. Calhoun of South Carolina, warned that because the balance of power between North and South was being destroyed, 'political revolution, anarchy, civil war, and widespread disaster' would inevitably result. Sadly his prediction was correct. Little more than a decade later, the most violent war in American history pitted brother against brother and almost destroyed the American Union.

The Mexican War provided a training ground for young officers who fought each other in the American Civil War, which broke out just 13 years after the signing of the Treaty of Guadalupe Hidalgo. More than 130 veterans of the armies of Taylor and Scott became generals in that conflict. Students of that war will recognize these names among others: for the North, Ulysses S. Grant, Joseph Hooker, George McClellan, and Don Carlos Buell; for the South, Robert E. Lee, Thomas (Stonewall) Jackson, Pierre Gustave Toutant Beauregard, James Longstreet, Braxton Bragg, and George Pickett. Unfortunately for the soldiers on both sides, their generals had learned the art of war all too well.

In the years between the wars, however, American commerce boomed as new canals were built to be plied by paddle-wheeled steamboats. Soon these would be challenged by the railroads. Mostly constructed by Irish laborers and financed by English capital, railroads spread across the eastern and northern states like giant spiders' webs, linking inland markets to the burgeoning seaports on the Atlantic coast.

This new, rapid means of transportation created increased commercial traffic between the United States and Europe. It opened up new fields of investment for capital-rich European banks, providing funds needed for the rapid growth of American industry.

As the railroads probed into the newly settled middle west, agricultural goods from that great granary no longer required transport to New Orleans by slow barges down the Mississippi River. From New Orleans they would have had to be loaded on ships for voyages to the American eastern seaboard or to Europe, a laborious and expensive method of transportation. Now, swift trains could ship goods quickly and cheaply to expanding eastern cities. Very soon, the dream of a coast-to-coast railroad system, crossing 3,000 miles from New York to the Pacific Ocean, would become a reality.

With ports like Seattle, San Francisco, San Diego, and Los Angeles now in American hands, the United States turned its eyes toward Asia, which offered the prospect of new and lucrative markets. Spanning a continent stretching from the Atlantic to the Pacific, the United States of America was poised to enter the stage of international affairs as a new world power.

Further reading

Chamberlain, Samuel E., *My Confession*, Harper (New York, 1956)

De Voto, Bernard, *Year of Decision 1846*, Houghton Mifflin (Boston, 1942)

Eisenhower, John, *So Far From God: The U.S. War with Mexico*, Random House (New York, 1989)

Frazier, Donald S., *The U.S. and Mexico at War*, Macmillan (New York, 1998)

Grant, Ulysses S., *Memoirs and Selected Letters*, The Library of America (1990)

Hamilton, Holman, *Zachary Taylor: Soldier of the Republic*, Archon Books (1941)

Johnson, Timothy D., *Winfield Scott: The Quest for Military Glory*, University Press of Kansas (1998)

Krauze, Enrique, *Mexico: Biography of Power*, Harpers (New York, 1997)

Lewis, Lloyd, *Captain Sam Grant*, Little & Brown (Boston, 1950)

Maverick, Mary Ann, *Memoirs of Mary A. Maverick*, Alamo Printing Company (San Antonio, Texas, 1921)

Meed, Douglas V., *The Fighting Texas Navy 1832–1843*, Republic of Texas Press (Plano, Texas, 2001)

Miller, Robert Ryal, *Shamrock and Sword: The Saint Patrick's Battalion in the U.S. – Mexican War*, University of Oklahoma Press (Norman, 1989)

Nevin, David, *The Mexican War*, Time-Life Books (Alexandria, Virginia, 1978)

Robinson, Cecil, *The View From Chapultepec: Mexican Writers on the Mexican-American War*, University of Arizona Press (Tucson, 1989)

Ruiz, Ramon Eduardo, *Triumph and Tragedy: A History of the Mexican People*, Norton (New York, 1992)

Smith, Page, *The Nation Comes of Age*, McGraw-Hill, (New York 1981)

Webb, Walter Prescott, *The Texas Rangers*, The University of Texas Press (Austin, 1935)

Weems, John Edward, *To Conquer A Peace*, Doubleday (Garden City, New York, 1974)

Weigley, Russell F., *The American Way of War*, Macmillan (New York, 1973)

Wilkins, Frederick, *The Highly Irregular Irregulars: Texas Rangers in the Mexican War*, Eakin Press (Austin, 1990)

Winders, Richard Price, *Mr. Polk's Army*, Texas A&M Press (College Station, 1997)

Index

Related titles from Osprey Publishing

CAMPAIGN (CAM)
Strategies, tactics and battle experiences of opposing armies

NEW VANGUARD (NVG)
Design, development and operation of the machinery of war
Contact us for more details – see below

WARRIOR (WAR)
Motivation, training, combat experiences and equipment of individual soldiers

ELITE (ELI)
Uniforms, equipment, tactics and personalities of troops and commanders

ESSENTIAL HISTORIES (ESS)
Concise overviews of major wars and theatres of war

ORDER OF BATTLE (OOB)
Unit-by-unit troop movements and command strategies of major battles
Contact us for more details – see below

MEN-AT-ARMS (MAA)
Uniforms, equipment, history and organisation of troops

To order any of these titles, or for more information on Osprey Publishing, contact:
Osprey Direct (UK) *Tel:* +44 (0)1933 443863 *Fax:* +44 (0)1933 443849 *E-mail:* info@ospreydirect.co.uk
Osprey Direct (USA) c/o MBI Publishing *Toll-free:* 1 800 826 6600 *Phone:* 1 715 294 3345
Fax: 1 715 294 4448 *E-mail:* info@ospreydirectusa.com
www.ospreypublishing.com